TALENT
UNLEASHED

TALENT
UNLEASHED

3 LEADERSHIP CONVERSATIONS TO IGNITE THE UNLIMITED POTENTIAL IN PEOPLE

SHAWN D. MOON | TODD DAVIS | MICHAEL SIMPSON | A. ROGER MERRILL

A POST HILL PRESS BOOK

Talent Unleashed:
3 Leadership Conversations to Ignite the Unlimited Potential in People
© 2017 by FranklinCovey
All Rights Reserved

ISBN: 978-1-68261-002-2
ISBN (eBook): 978-1-68261-003-9

Cover Design by The Creative Lab at FranklinCovey
Interior Design and Composition by Greg Johnson/Textbook Perfect

Post Hill

PRESS

Post Hill Press
posthillpress.com

Published in the United States of America

ACKNOWLEDGEMENTS

A project like this comes to fruition only as a result of countless peoples' efforts. We express first our most sincere gratitude for the wonderful clients we've been able to work with and serve. Their commitment to leadership, to creating something powerful and meaningful within their teams and organizations, is nothing short of inspiring. Our clients' willingness to work, to change, to challenge, to partner, and to be vulnerable has provided—and continues to provide—new insights and direction. Thank you for this remarkable privilege!

We acknowledge the ongoing contributions of our colleagues, including senior delivery consultants, practice leaders, general managers, client partners, administrative partners, and the FranklinCovey executive team. Their undying support and thought leadership brings new insights every day in how to hold effective leadership conversations.

Special gratitude goes to Stephanie Bexfield, Annie Oswald, Jill White, Jody Karr and the entire Creative Lab at Franklin-Covey, Tiffani Lindsey, Alicia Cunningham, Adam Merrill, Sean Covey, Catherine Nelson, Bob Whitman, and the inestimable Breck England, without whose efforts this book would never have happened. Many thanks to Rebecca Merrill for her extensive hours and incredible expertise. She has given voice and cohesion to an otherwise disjointed aggregation of ideas and research.

Our personal and professional lives have forever been shaped by our association with the late Dr. Stephen R. Covey. His contributions continue to ripple across the world.

Finally, we thank our families. Stephen R. Covey once defined leadership as "communicating to people their worth and potential so clearly that they come to see it in themselves." Thank you for your willingness to see, communicate, and encourage what we often couldn't see in ourselves. Your boundless love and unflagging support is the reason any of this happens.

CONTENTS

A Note About the Text: We are sharing our personal stories as "Author Notes" so you can focus on the story rather than on who is telling the story.

UNLEASHING TALENT

Most leaders and employees do not know what their strengths are. When you ask them, they look at you with a blank stare, or they respond to you in terms of subject knowledge—which is the wrong answer.

—PETER DRUCKER

It was rush hour on a cold January morning. The Washington, D.C., Metro was bustling with early commuters racing to catch their trains, focused on maintaining their schedules, and hoping to make it to work on time. In the midst of the rush, a man sat down on the freezing cement, perfectly positioned in a corridor where all the travelers had to pass by him on their way.

In his hands, the man held a violin case. He opened it, removed the violin from its protective padding, and placed the case in front of him, silently asking for listeners to throw in a dollar or two. Or twenty...or more.

This anonymous violinist then began to play. He had chosen six Johann Sebastian Bach compositions to perform for the morning travelers. His playing was flawless, but few noticed. After several minutes, a middle-aged man paused for a moment. But after less than a minute, he moved on. The musician received his first contribution several minutes later as a woman tossed a dollar into his open violin case, but she didn't slow her determined pace. A few minutes later, an older gentleman paused for a moment as he leaned against the Metro station wall. But he soon looked at his watch and hurried along to his destination as well.

The man played for about 45 minutes, and in that time thousands of commuters passed in front of him. Children seemed to have the most interest in his music. The first person who looked like he wanted to stay and listen was a three-year-old boy, who seemed mesmerized both by the music and the musician. But his mother clearly had places to go and dragged him forward. Many other children stopped to listen, and without exception, their parents prodded them ahead, never slowing to take in the performance even for a moment.

When he was done, the violinist gathered his donations, packed up his instrument, snapped the case closed, and left. In the 45 minutes, he had collected $32 in his violin case. There was no applause or recognition for his effort. There was nothing but the morning rush—the process of getting the daily commute over so that important work could begin.

The event was a social experiment conducted by *The Washington Post*. The man who played in the cold station that morning was Joshua Bell, one of the world's finest violinists. He performed six of the most complex and intricate pieces ever composed for the violin, and he did it on an instrument that was worth $3.5 million. Just two nights earlier, Bell had performed to a sold-out concert hall in Boston, where tickets averaged more than $100.

It seems almost unimaginable that nearly every one of the thousands of people who rushed past Joshua Bell that day could be completely oblivious of the demonstration of his world-class talent. Yet, how often do we walk past magnificent talent that might be right before our eyes?

Like the people at the Metro station, we often ignore great-ness and brilliance simply because we are not fully present in the here and now. We get so busy in the urgent press of the day, consumed with getting things done or going somewhere, that we ignore—or at the very least, give less-than-passing acknowledgement to—the extraordinary talent that is almost always before us.

How often do you see the talents of those you associate with?

How often are you aware of the unique gifts of those who surround you?

As a leader, do you have even a glimmering of the poten-tial in the people on your team? Do you even see the talent in yourself?

Not only are we talking about that wicked outside basket-ball shot you swooshed last Friday. Or the fact that you can speak four languages. Or the 24 hot yoga moves you've mastered.

We're talking about the vast, hidden resources in yourself and others that have never been tapped or even suspected. We're talking about the "Joshua Bell" within your team members and within you.

Think about this: Have you ever had a leader in your life identify a capacity within you that you yourself did not see?

If so, how did it affect your life?

How did it affect your relationships with others?

Would you like to be able to do for others what this person did for you?

> **AUTHOR NOTE** As a teenager, I was about as lazy as one can get. I was a poor student—I got lousy grades even in subjects I was good at. History, for example. I actually loved history and read a lot of it on my own, but I refused to read my schoolbooks. That was work!

One day my history teacher, who I thought didn't like me at all, pulled me aside after class and looked me in the eye. He said to me in a shaky voice, "You are shortchanging yourself. You could do so much better. In fact, I think you have a gift for history."

As he said those words, I had a strange feeling inside. No teacher had ever shown any particular interest in me before. Gradually, I shaped up under his eye. He watched me, coached me, and kept encouraging me. His vision of what I could do inspired me, and I began to work. To cut to the chase, I eventually graduated with first-class honors in history from a major university. It was a great feeling, and I owe my success in large part to that one teacher with a shaky voice who cared.

In contrast, an associate of ours shared the following experience:

I once worked with a senior leader who felt that developing people, really investing in them, took up too much time and eventually led to disappointment. He said to me, "You spend all that time and money developing them, and then, once they have learned what they need to know, they leave."

I empathized with him. It certainly can be frustrating to invest in people and then have them choose to go elsewhere. But then I said to him, "Let's look at this a little differently. What if you don't invest in them, and they stay? What kind of people would you be working with then?"

This leader lacked the spirit to keep great people. He saw time investing in his people as a waste, and then felt resentful when they left.

Leadership today requires many things, but one of the fundamental roles of a great leader is to see, recognize, and ultimately unleash the talents and strengths of others—and to create a bonding attraction for these people to the organizations for which they work so these talents and strengths are not developed and then lost to others in today's rapidly changing work environment.

So how do leaders do that? Think about it. While most leaders are promoted for their competence and skills, truly exceptional leaders are remembered for the impact they have on the lives of those they lead. When you ask people to tell you about the best leader they've ever had (and we have—on six continents around the world), they rarely will say that this leader was the most technically competent person they ever met. Rather, they will tell you about this person's humanity, courage, concern, and deep personal interest—about how he or she helped people grow, develop, accomplish tasks, and find greater meaning in work and contribution.

They will tell you that this leader genuinely cared.

More than 80 percent of those we asked said that at least two of the following statements describe the "greatest leader" they have ever worked for.

- ▸ "I had confidence that my leader would help me discover, develop, and use my talents in order to accomplish something meaningful."
- ▸ "I had confidence that we shared a vision of what I was to accomplish, why it was important, and how I was going to do it."
- ▸ "I had confidence that my leader would be seeking ways to be a source of help to me."

In today's work environment, creating that kind of confidence is not just "nice to do"; it is absolutely critical for attracting and retaining top talent and creating high performance. True, there's a price for taking the time to create the relationships that inspire growth, creativity, top performance, and loyalty to leaders and organizations, but the payoff can be enormous.

You've probably heard it said that people don't leave organizations, they leave managers. You've also probably heard it said that "Millennials" (generally considered those born between the early 1980s and sometime around the year 2000) are the most mobile generation ever, frequently hopping from one job to another. In fact, Gallup reports that Millennials—who now make up more than half the workforce in the United States[1]—are the most likely generation to switch jobs, with 60 percent open to a new job opportunity.[2]

But it's our experience that good people in all generations (Millennials, Gen-Xers, Boomers, and Silents) generally don't leave involved managers who genuinely care about them and create an inclusive work environment. People in every demographic want connection. They want to feel like they belong and that their leaders and team members genuinely care about them. They want to feel that they have the help and support of their leaders in accomplishing important goals and making meaningful contributions. Managers and leaders who inspire these kinds of connections often make the difference between success and demise for organizations.

This book is about 3 Leadership Conversations that can enable you—as a leader of a team, a project, or an organization—to create that sense of caring and belonging. It's about how they can help you attract and keep the best and brightest and unleash their talent toward what matters most. It's about how they can make it possible for you to create the connection and the confidence described in the three bullet points above.

We recognize there are many opportunities for leadership in today's world—both formal and informal. In our team-oriented, flexible workplace, you may be the leader of a team one day and report to a team member on a different project the next. You may also have opportunities to mentor and coach. However, we suggest that all of these opportunities fall under the umbrella of leadership, and these conversations can effectively be woven throughout all of these interactions and roles.

Initially, you can learn how to conduct these conversations in a matter of moments and create immediate positive results. Over time, however, you can develop a rich resource of knowledge, character, and skill to create an environment of leadership conversation in your team or organization that will fully unleash talent and clear the path for high performance.

Although the focus of this book is on using these conversations to create top business and organizational performance, as you can tell from some of our personal sharing—and probably your own thoughts as you read—these conversations are also extremely helpful in interacting with family members and others with whom we have important relationships and informal leadership influence.

Our promise to you is this:

If you will engage with us by reading this book and begin to hold genuine Leadership Conversations with those around you using the Conversation Guides throughout the book, you will:

- ▶ Develop a new leadership mindset and skillset that will significantly strengthen your relationships with those you lead.
- ▶ Develop confidence in your ability to recognize and unleash the talents of others.
- ▶ Develop a growing awareness that as you unleash the talents of others, you are unleashing your own as well.

Talent Unleashed is a collaborative work by four authors who have seen firsthand the success of leaders worldwide who unleash the talents of those around them. We will occasionally share with you a few of these leaders' stories. But most of this book is based on the work we have collectively done with literally thousands of FranklinCovey clients over the past 30 years.

The answer was clear. *It is leaders who unleash the talent of those with whom they work.*

The ability to unleash talent grows out of how leaders see people and their potential and how they interact with those they lead. Effective leaders genuinely respect and care about people—about their personal growth and the meaning they get from their work, as well as their contributions to the team or organization. As a result, the people they lead are motivated to discover and unleash their talents and to give their very best.

This caring is not a leadership fad or technique. In fact, it has been recognized as an integral part of effective leadership throughout history. One of the oldest manuscripts known—"The Maxims of Ptahhotep" (ca. 2200 BCE)—is a good example.

Ptahhotep was a city administrator and vizier (first minister) in Egypt during the reign of Djedkare Isesi in the Fifth Dynasty. He is credited with authoring this early piece of Egyptian "wisdom literature," which was meant to instruct young men in appropriate behavior. From the content of the manuscript, we learn that Ptahhotep placed great value on people and their talents and capacities. Since the book you're reading is about the 3 Leadership *Conversations*, it is particularly interesting to note that the literal translation of the Ptahhotep document is "The Maxims of Good Discourse."

With a few changes to update the language, some of the wisdom of this leader could well have come from the latest management and leadership literature. For example, this is what Ptahhotep had to say about the importance of listening (and therefore demonstrating caring) to those you lead:

> If you are to be a leader, be patient in your hearing when the petitioner speaks, do not halt him until his belly is emptied of what he had planned to say.... Not everything for which he petitions can come to be, but a good hearing is soothing for the heart.[2]

At one point or another, it becomes evident to most people that *good* leaders genuinely do care about the people they lead. Perhaps less evident—or at least less articulated—is the reality that truly *great* leaders not only care about people, they also *manifest* that caring in ways that really matter and make a difference to those around them.

As the four of us began to examine our own practical experience and global research, our efforts to discover the most effective ways of communicating caring eventually led us to boil our findings down to 3 Leadership Conversations—rich, ongoing discussions among leaders and those they lead—that result in the recognition and unleashing of talent.

In each case, these conversations communicate sincere caring for the individual. On an ongoing basis, they maximize the opportunity to bring success, joy, and fulfillment to individuals and dramatically improved performance to teams and organizations.

The purpose of this book is to share with you these 3 Leadership Conversations—what they are, why they work, and how to develop the practical skills to create them. In doing this, we will share with you a practical tool—some simple Conversation Guides—that can enable anyone to begin to conduct these conversations immediately.

Leadership Is a Conversation

It's been said, "Marriage is just one long conversation, so make sure you marry someone you like talking to!" In reality, all good relationships are really just a series of healthy conversations. The more meaningful, trusting, and open the conversation, the more rewarding the relationship.

As leadership experts Robert J. Anderson and William A. Adams point out, "leadership [too] is a conversation."[3]

Leaders spend most of their days in conversation—meetings, phone calls, emails, and strategic communications. How you show up in these conversations determines your level of effectiveness.... The quality of the leadership conversations determines collective effectiveness, which determines collective intelligence, which determines business performance.... The quality of our conversation and our relationships correlates directly with the results we create.[4]

So if leadership is really one long conversation—and we're communicating all the time—it might be helpful to think about the nature of our conversation with those with whom we work. We might ask ourselves, "Is my conversation generous, honest, helpful, motivating, and encouraging people to better and more purposeful contribution—in other words, does it really communicate caring? Or is it rare, perfunctory, emotionally flat, and always focused only on the task at hand? Even worse, is it dreaded, down-in-the-mouth critical, and caustic?"

Figure 1.1 has excerpts from some typical workplace communication. Think about the implication of what is being communicated and think about the results. From your own experience, can you think of other recent examples where what was said communicated unintended but powerful messages?

Think about your own communication. What do the words you speak to those you lead reveal about your mindset regarding your team, your organization, and your own role? And what is the result in your team or organization?

As we work with people in organizations around the world, we often hear comments such as these:

- ▶ "I don't understand our goals, if we even have any."
- ▶ "The vision, direction, and purposes of our team are unclear to me."

THE 3 LEADERSHIP CONVERSATIONS

FIGURE 1.1

What Was Said	What Was Communicated
"Well, if you understood the reasoning coming from the head office, you'd be on the executive committee. So let's just get it done, okay?"	Your ideas are not valued. You're not a person; you're just a part of a machine run by smarter and better people than you.
"It's just that there are good companies and bad companies—there is very little we can do about it."	We are victims. There's nothing we can do to change our situation.
"The good people are leaving and the low performers are staying."	This is a bad place to work. If you stay here, you are a "low performer" and don't really have any other choice.
"I hope you've got somebody to back up what you're saying, or you're going to get hammered."	Hide bad news. Personal survival demands it. We can't be open, honest, or transparent here.
"Those people in shipping just don't get it. They are operating in a vacuum."	The problem is not with us. The problem is "out there." They are the ones who should be blamed.
"The cuts are so deep that we don't even have the time or capability to do our own job."	We can't possibly succeed—but it's not our fault.
"Did you hear that Marcie over in the Operations group was just let go after 15 years? This organization seems to chew people up and spit them out."	You need to fear for your job. Those who lead are not loyal to us (and, by implication, do not deserve our loyalty).
"After we worked so long on that project, corporate is not supporting it at all. They just don't understand what a great opportunity this is."	We don't know or trust what we're expected to accomplish in our job. Upper management is incompetent and clueless. We're sunk.
"There's never enough time or resources to do the job right the first time. But there's plenty of time to go back and criticize everybody for not doing it right."	We're at the mercy of unreasonable people who are either too dumb or too greedy to provide us what we need.

▶ "I sometimes wonder if what we do is even recognized or if it really makes a difference in the long run."

▶ "I don't know what significant contribution I can make in my role."

▶ "I don't have the power to make my own decisions about my work."

▶ "I don't feel like anyone listens to me. Why would they?"

▶ "I often feel that my boss is more concerned about protecting himself or looking good than really solving the problem."

What motivation do people who feel like this have to discover and give their best?

Now consider the great leaders you've known. What was their "leadership by conversation" like? Did those they led have such a lack of clarity regarding their team's or organization's purpose or about their own talents or roles? Were they this apathetic about contributing?

Successful leaders, coaches, and mentors deeply care about and unleash the talents of those around them, tapping their passion, energy, and commitment. Their leadership conversations engage the whole person—the mind, the spirit, and the heart. And these conversations have a huge impact on engagement.

According to a *Gallup Business Journal* report: "managers account for up to 70 percent of variance in engagement," and, interestingly, "consistent *communication* is connected to higher engagement." Specifically, "engagement is highest among employees who have some form (face-to-face, phone, or digital) of daily communication with their managers" and "clarity of expectations is perhaps the most basic of employee needs and is vital to performance.... Great managers don't just tell employees what's expected of them and leave it at that; instead, they frequently talk with employees about their responsibilities and progress. They don't save those critical conversations for once-a-year performance reviews."[5]

The 3 Leadership Conversations we describe in this book provide a cultural framework for creating and improving your own leadership conversations to help you communicate more deliberately and clearly. They also help you communicate caring in ways that make a significant positive difference. In conducting these conversations, leaders create trust, recognize performance, establish expectations, and constantly refine and refocus strategic purpose.

Voice, Performance, and Clearing the Path

Our research and experience have led us to conclude that the most important leadership conversations are about:

1. "Voice" or contribution.
2. Performance on vital goals.
3. Clearing the path to progress.

FIGURE 1.2

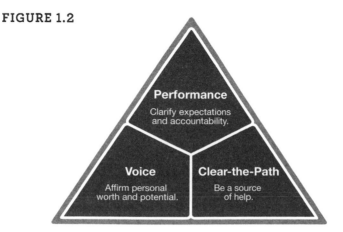

1. **Voice Conversations** affirm the worth and potential of each person on a team. In a Voice Conversation, individuals discover their unique talents, passions, and values—their individual "voice"—and align these to their job and career responsibilities. It is the process of identifying an individual's unique talents and contribution.

2. **Performance Conversations** establish and clarify goals, targets, roles, responsibilities, and accountability. In a Performance Conversation, individuals are transformed from "interchangeable employees" to trusted partners, colleagues, and teammates who work together to accomplish goals that are vital to individual and organizational performance.

3. **Clear-the-Path Conversations** turn supervisors into leaders, coaches, and mentors who become sources of help, enabling people to succeed in their jobs. Leaders "clear the path" by removing obstacles, teaching, coaching, and making course corrections along the way.

These conversations are the work of effective leaders distilled down to its essence. Voice Conversations help team members define their unique talents and contributions. Performance Conversations clarify expectations and recognize achievement. Clear-the-Path Conversations help identify what team members and leaders can do to remove obstacles and help facilitate success.

In reality, the 3 Leadership Conversations are really just parts of the one long Leadership Conversation focused into small connections you can create at any time. Some of these conversations will be longer and more formal; many will be short and seemingly spur-of-the-moment. By utilizing this framework, you as a leader can ensure you don't squander meaningful moments with your people—moments when you can listen for voice, focus on performance, and find ways to clear the path.

Many of the conversations will happen live; however, in today's world, many will also happen virtually—through email, texts, and social media. Face-to-face matters. Nothing replaces the connection of live human beings. But technology can offer us many more opportunities to connect, and sometimes to share more personal or difficult thoughts and ideas.

These Leadership Conversations create inflection points for people. Lives are transformed by a sense of mission. Important goals are set and accomplished. People gain hope as they realize their leader is always available to help people along the journey. As a result, individuals and teams are enabled to give and coordinate their best efforts for a remarkable sense of shared success and personal joy and fulfillment in their work.

The conversations are about improving the performance of the team or organization by bringing out the best that people can contribute. But just as important, they're about the "how"—about building the caring relationships without which any positive leadership conversation will not work.

As brain scientist Edward M. Hallowell has said:

> The all-powerful propeller of connection begins with a link to a particular person, then grows. It becomes sustaining and ever-present, a feeling of being a part of something positive that is larger than yourself, a feeling that life is workable no matter what bad things come up. This is the one force that, above all others, brings out the best in people.[6]

This personal connection demonstrates caring. The importance of this connection has been brought out cleverly in a twist on the "Big Rocks" demonstration FranklinCovey presenters have used for years to teach an important principle of time management. This version is referred to as "the story of the mayonnaise jar and the two cups of coffee."

A college professor stood before his class with a huge, empty mayonnaise jar. When class began, wordlessly, he began filling the jar with golf balls.

He asked the students if the jar was full. They agreed that it was.

The professor then picked up a box of pebbles and poured it into the jar. He shook the jar lightly. The pebbles rolled into the open areas between the golf balls.

He then asked the students again if the jar was full. They agreed it was.

The professor next picked up a box of sand and poured it into the jar. Of course, the sand filled up everything else.

He asked once again if the jar was full. The students responded with a unanimous "Yes."

The professor then produced two cups of coffee from under the table and poured the entire contents into the jar. The students laughed.

"Now," said the professor, as the laughter subsided, "I want you to recognize that this jar represents your life. The golf balls stand for the people you love and care for. If everything else was lost and only they remained, your life would still be full.

"The pebbles are other things that matter, like your job or your home. The sand is everything else—the small stuff.

"If you put the sand into the jar first, there is no room for the pebbles or the golf balls. The same goes for life. If you spend all your time and energy on the small stuff, you will never have room for the things that are most important to you.

"So pay attention to the things that are critical to your happiness. Spend your energy on the people you love and care about. Take time to listen to them—to teach, guide, and encourage them. Show them you love them. Set your priorities. Take care of the golf balls first, then the pebbles. The rest is just sand."

A student then raised her hand and asked what the coffee represented. The professor smiled and said, "I'm glad you asked. It just goes to show that no matter how full your life may seem, there's always room for a couple of cups of coffee with a friend."

Why Great Leaders Care About Caring

Successful leaders care about people, unleashing the talents of those around them and tapping their passion, energy, and commitment. Unsuccessful bosses, on the other hand, are invested in their own credit and their own positions of authority and power. The question we need to ask ourselves is, "Where is my locus of caring? Is it focused on myself—or on others?"

AUTHOR NOTE Very early in my career, I worked for a man who never gave up control of anything. If power were a pie, he wanted the entire pie—with the ice cream. He did not allow for innovation, experimentation, or the development of talent around him because he feared somebody else might get some recognition. Every day was an exercise in boredom as we tried to come up with new ways to stay busy and out of his way.

Just consider the impact of that kind of self-focus on the morale, engagement, and productivity of those who worked under this man's "leadership."

Great leaders don't worry about credit. They focus instead on caring and communicating that caring—and on creating new opportunities, developing future talent, and leaving a legacy of leadership. They view their role as building other leaders, and they do this by amply sharing the credit with those who have done the work.

And their language reflects those paradigms and values. They talk about "we" instead of "me." They share the pie. And the ice cream. And everyone enjoys the results.

Let us share with you an example of the results of that kind of caring.

Toward the end of the 19th century, American industrialist Henry Ford was a young entrepreneur with a great dream: he wanted to build an affordable automobile that was within the budgetary reach of almost every family. He knew he had to find a way to get the price down to about what it would cost to buy a horse and buggy. His idea was ridiculed by many. But he didn't stop. Needing financial support, he went to J.P. Morgan's bank, the biggest American bank, and asked for a loan. His request was denied.

Disheartened and unsure how to proceed, Ford discussed his ideas with his boss, Thomas A. Edison. Edison recognized the talent in Ford and said, "Young man, that's the thing! You have it—the self-contained unit carrying its own fuel with it! Keep at it!"[7] Those words of encouragement changed everything for Ford and changed everything for the world. Although his first two tries failed, Ford finally created and released the very first Model A Ford, which became very popular. He gave the first car out of the factory to Edison.

Edison's caring and personal touch stoked the fire that made Ford successful. For years they—and other innovators—went camping together, sharing ideas, fiddling around with new inventions, and just talking. These conversations gave Ford the courage to follow through on his dream, even after multiple failures.

Is there someone in your life who cared enough to make that personal connection and take time just to talk with you, inspire you, teach you—even correct you sometimes?

Was it a teacher? A coach? A friend? Perhaps it was a family member, your first boss, or even a colleague in your office. This leader may not necessarily have been someone who filled a "formal" leadership role. It could simply have been someone who took an interest in you, and more particularly, took time with you—someone who saw talent in you waiting to be unleashed, as Edison did with Ford.

> My definition of leadership is communicating to people their worth and potential so clearly that they are inspired to see it in themselves.
>
> —STEPHEN R. COVEY

If you've had such a leader in your life, you might have even felt the sting of gentle (or not so gentle) reproof from time to time, but you always felt that person's concern for you. You knew that person wanted the best for you. You knew he or she believed in you. You wanted to live up to that individual's standard. You understood that accountability was high and perhaps so was the possibility you would fail before you ever achieved anything noteworthy; but you also understood that this leader was there to support you in your efforts, remove barriers in order to clear your path to success, and continue to raise the bar for you.

Over the years, we have asked leaders in thousands of business audiences, "Who have been the great leaders in your life?"

For the most part, these business leaders can answer instantly. Generally, they think of someone who genuinely cared about them, and saw and communicated their worth and potential so clearly to them that they began to see it in themselves—someone who was able to unleash their talent.

One of our associates shared this story of a leader who unleashed his capacities:

It was my teacher. I was in a troubled-youth program. I had no sense of perspective for who I was or what I could possibly accomplish. He sat me down one day—not as part of a scheduled meeting or as part of some punishment, just in the normal course of the day. He looked at me and asked, very simply but sincerely, "What would you like to do in your life?" In a more confrontational environment, I might have taken offense to the question. But that was not the spirit of his intent, and I immediately felt his genuine interest. I said something lame like, "Uh, I don't know." He then looked piercingly at me and said, "You can be or do anything you want. You have tremendous capability and an amazing amount of talent, and I know you will do significant things in your life."

I was struck speechless. I had never seen myself making even small contributions, let alone great ones. I didn't think I even cared until that moment. But he had just told me I could do great things, and I believed him.

I began, at that moment, to see myself and my capabilities differently because I was willing to see myself as he saw me. And though I still had my occasional stumbles, I began to behave in alignment with that vision. Over the years, I kept in close contact with this man, who became a mentor to me. He was sometimes stern with me. He held me responsible for the consequences of my actions. But at the same time, he continued to help me expand my vision of who I was and what I could do, explore my interests and dreams, and remove barriers along the way.

As I look back on where I was and what I have since accomplished, I am amazed at the journey and the path I began to take that day. I graduated from high school, earned a college degree (the first in my family to do so), then a master's degree. I married a wonderful person. I have a terrific family. I have enjoyed professional success, and today I am the leader of a large team of very talented people that does very important work. It hasn't always been easy, but I have, in fact, done some significant things. And I will forever be grateful to my friend who first inspired me with a short but sincere conversation.

More of us need to be leaders who influence others to better performance. We need to care about people for one reason, because it's simply the moral thing for human beings to do. For another reason, it brings great happiness to us as well as others. But in addition, there's also a very good business reason for caring.

> Consciously or subconsciously, people decide how much of themselves they will give to their work depending on how they are treated.... These choices range from rebelling or quitting to creative excitement.
>
> —STEPHEN R. COVEY

The value of human resources has become the chief determinant of the value of an enterprise. In the 1980s, Standard & Poor's assigned about a third of the value of a firm to "intangible assets"; that is, "the credibility of leadership and the quality and talent of the people."[8] Now, decades later, intangible assets count for as much as 84 percent of the market value of the S&P 500 companies.[9]

As Narayana Murthy, cofounder of Infosys, so memorably put it, "Our most important assets walk out of the door each evening. We have to make sure that they come back the next morning."[10]

Investors are deeply interested in the people you lead: Who are they? What can they do? How's their morale, their engagement, their passion? What's the quality of their leadership?[11]

> What is the biggest management mistake that management makes? They treat people like commodities.
> They treat people like numbers, not like people. It is just that simple.
>
> —CLAY MATHILE

It's often easy for leaders, particularly in business, to obsess over one segment of the market value—the financials—while essentially neglecting the people who *create* that value. It's easy for all of us to become "too busy," to become blinded to the value of others by a false sense of our own self-importance, to become lazy, or to get caught up in the "control" paradigm trying to manage everyone and everything, so we don't have the deep, meaningful conversations that unleash the talent and motivation of others.

The four of us often come in contact with managers and leaders who really feel they care about "their people" and believe these people know it. But in talking with these people, we discover this is often a delusion.

As leaders, we don't want to be deluded. We don't want to be like the man who said of his wife of many years, "When we were first married, I told her I loved her. I never felt the need to say those words again. If my feelings had changed, I would have told her."

So, what can we do? How can we ensure that we exercise the kind of leadership that demonstrates sincere caring and ignites talent?

The key is in the nature and quality of our leadership conversations.

What You Can Expect from This Book

The next three chapters of this book explore the 3 Leadership Conversations in depth and describe how you can conduct each of these conversations successfully. Starting with the Voice Conversation, you can learn how to help each team member recognize his or her own unique talents and discover (and become impassioned by) the powerful contribution he or she can make. In the Performance Conversation, you can learn how to help each individual create meaningful goals for realizing that contribution. In the Clear-the-Path Conversation, you can learn how to teach and coach people and remove the obstacles to success.

Although you can hold any of the conversations anytime, most people find the sequence in which we've presented them the most helpful, especially in the beginning. Thereafter, these conversations can be held based on need, and elements of each of the conversations can be effectively woven into almost any verbal interaction. In fact, the goal of an effective leader is not only to understand and hold *formal* conversations in each of these three areas, but to create the environment in which *informal* conversations in these areas take place naturally every day.

The key is to always keep the *context* of effective leadership conversation in mind—in other words, to say whatever you say in the framework of helping the person strengthen his or her "voice" and passion to contribute, develop excellence and confidence in performance, and have as clear a path as possible to success.

In each of these next three chapters, you will find visuals of the Conversation Guides we referred to earlier in the chapter. Copies of all the guides are in the Appendix at the back of this book. We use these guides in our executive coaching and training. They contain the key questions that drive each conversation.

In each chapter, we've included a number of additional questions you can ask to give yourself deeper understanding of the content and options for dealing with specific issues and areas of focus; however, the questions on the guides are the ones that are fundamental in actually holding the conversations. The guides also contain "watchouts"—pitfalls to avoid when holding each conversation.

When you engage in the 3 Leadership Conversations— and particularly when you're just beginning—we encourage you to share copies of the guides with those with whom you are engaging. Don't hesitate to explain, "As we talk together today, I'm going to be using a guide that has some questions we may find helpful. Here's a copy for you. Let's look at these together and see what we can discover." One of the benefits of using the guides is that the very process is transparent. It communicates openness and trust. In essence, it says: "Here is what I'm looking at. You're looking at the same thing. Let's make this happen together."

As helpful as these guides are to most people, keep in mind that they are just tools. You don't have to use them. Your own ideas to apply the principles behind them may work just as well. So as long as you understand the principles, use whatever works for you. In Chapter 5, you'll find a review of the foundational principles associated with the conversations. You'll see how understanding and applying the natural laws of contribution, trust, and synergy can unleash human talent, even in the face of everyday challenges and pressures.

At the end of each chapter, you'll find a set of searching discussion questions. We suggest you ponder these questions and talk through them with your team or someone else you trust. You can also use the questions to discuss with your team what unleashing talent can mean to them as individuals, to the team as a whole, and to the company or organization you work for. You will likely find it helpful to answer these questions for yourself if you aspire to lead an "unleashed" team.

The rest of this book is essentially an in-depth explanation and exploration of the content of the Conversation Guides. Using the guides makes holding these conversations very simple. In fact, you can begin to use them immediately with positive results. However, the following chapters provide levels of understanding and application that will greatly enrich your experience and significantly multiply the value of the conversations in helping you and your team achieve top performance. We hope you find this book useful and enjoy holding these vital Leadership Conversations with the members of your team. (See Appendix A for the Leadership Conversation cards.)

DISCUSSION QUESTIONS

1. According to this chapter, what is the profile of a great leader? In what ways might this profile apply to some of the great leaders you have known?

2. In your opinion, which is more important—getting a task done, or caring about the people who are doing it?

3. What does it mean to say that "leadership is a conversation"?

4. What might the benefits of holding Leadership Conversations be to you and your organization? In what ways do you think the 3 Leadership Conversations are central to unleashing talent?

5. In what ways might unleashing others' talents enable you to also unleash your own?

6. What does it mean to say you are communicating with your team, even when you say nothing?
7. What would happen if leaders treated those they lead like their most valuable assets instead of necessary expenses?
8. Why do you think the sequence of the 3 Leadership Conversations might be important? Can you think of circumstances when needs might be better met by changing the sequence?

CHAPTER 2

THE VOICE CONVERSATION

Who you are, what your values are, what you stand for....
They are your anchor, your guiding North Star. You won't
find them in a book. You'll find them in your soul.

—ANN MULCAHY

AUTHOR NOTE My phone rang early one Saturday morning. My caller ID told me that David, a good friend with whom I worked closely, was on the line. I answered quickly.

Unfortunately, David didn't have good news.

"I wanted to let you know that I've decided to take a new job."

David told me he'd been offered the job some time ago. He and his family had been considering the offer and what it would mean for all of them if he accepted.

Still torn, he had decided to ask his supervisor, Margaret, for her advice. He trusted her expertise, valued her opinion, and wanted to hear what she thought about the new offer.

"She tore me apart," David reported to me. "She was offended that I would even consider leaving. Before I talked to her, I was having a really hard time convincing myself to leave. Not anymore."

Hoping David could still be saved, I called Margaret. Before I even said hello, Margaret made a confession.

"It's about David, right? I have really messed up," she said. "I'm going to talk with him again first thing Monday morning," she told me.

Margaret did sit down, and for three hours held what I would call a sincere Voice Conversation with David. She listened to him. She asked him about his hopes for his future and his family.

They talked about his talents and how they ought to be leveraged. They discussed his current job and compared it to the new opportunity. She asked him where he felt he could best "find his voice"—that "sweet spot" where his talents, passions, and opportunities might come together.

The relationship was salvaged and, thankfully, so were the services of our talented colleague. David felt heard; he felt understood; he was inspired to stay.

Today David is still with the company and happy to be there. He loves his work, and he loves his team. What a shame it would have been to lose his great talent. Luckily, Margaret humbly took a step back and arranged a Voice Conversation that made all the difference.

People want to be engaged in work that is meaningful. In fact, most of the people that managers and leaders really want on their teams put meaning and purpose first. They consider a good compensation package a minimum requirement; but even with one that is less than ideal, what they're really interested in is work that makes a difference.

In the mid-1900s, American psychologist Abraham Maslow published his famous hierarchy of needs, in which he argued that people must have their physical needs met before they will pay any attention to "self-actualization," or fulfilling their human potential. Research and experience show that this is only partially true. The world is filled with people who put higher purposes before even some important physical needs. When people are truly engaged in a cause they consider more important than anything else, they will make heavy sacrifices, even their physical well-being.

Of course, we don't need to—nor should we—ask team members to make that kind of sacrifice. But we do need to recognize that *meaning* is vitally important to people—often more important than other serious considerations.

Dartmouth College researcher Sydney Finkelstein lists *meaning and purpose* as the top factor in job satisfaction. "Go big on meaning," he says. "Most employees value jobs that let them contribute and make a difference, and many organizations now emphasize meaning and purpose in the hopes of fostering engagement."[1]

When a person discovers that contribution—that singular way of making a difference that is uniquely theirs to make—we call it "finding your voice."

In this chapter, we'll discuss the first of the 3 Leadership Conversations—the Voice Conversation. The purpose of this conversation is for the leader to hear, understand, and affirm the "voice" of each of those he or she leads, and to find the place where this voice best fits for the benefit of the individual and the organization. (See Figure 2.1.)

FIGURE 2.1

You *Are* Your Voice

You likely have friends who don't need to tell you who they are when they call you on the phone. You know who they are right away, even without a custom ring or caller ID. You know their *voice.*

You are in your voice. Your voice is unique. There is no voice like it anywhere else. It's more than just the vibration of your physical vocal cords—it's the communication of the whole combination of body, heart, mind, and spirit that makes *you.*

> **AUTHOR NOTE** When I think about how I gained any confidence at all in my own life and purpose, I think about my mother. For my first 18 years, hers was the first voice I heard when I woke up and the last voice I heard before going to sleep. She encouraged me to dream, to explore, to say yes to myself and to the future.
>
> I really appreciate having her constant, positive voice so early in my life. And to this day, I still hear her reassuring and optimistic voice, especially in those times when I have troubles or something exciting is going on. I know that voice, and it lifts me.

Some of the most meaningful conversations we ever have with others are about who we are and what we live for. Many of us have never had those kinds of conversations because we've never known anyone we felt we could trust enough to share with in such depth. We've never opened up what is deepest within us, what we yearn for most, and what really matters to us. For many of us, no one ever hears our voice.

And that's a tragedy. That's one of the fundamental reasons much human potential goes to waste.

Dr. Stephen R. Covey used to ask thousands of people who came to hear him speak this question: "How many of you agree that most people in your organization have far more passion, knowledge, talent, and capability to contribute than their current jobs require or even allow?" In nearly every instance, every hand would go up.

As Dr. Covey pointed out, great leaders have always helped others "find their voice." In his book *The 8ᵗʰ Habit: From Effectiveness to Greatness*, he tells the story of the man who helped him find *his* voice.

As a youth doing volunteer work, Dr. Covey was invited by his leader—a much older, more experienced man—to take on a staggering new job. In Dr. Covey's words:

> His confidence, his ability to see more in me than I saw in myself, his willingness to entrust me with a responsibility that would stretch me to my potential unlocked something inside me. I accepted the assignment and gave my best. It tapped me physically, mentally, emotionally, spiritually. I grew. I saw others grow. I saw patterns in basic leadership principles.... I had begun to detect the work I wanted to devote my life to: unleashing human potential. I found my "voice." And it was my leader that inspired me to find it.[2]

According to the Deloitte 2016 Millennial Survey, 44 percent of millennials said that within the next two years, they would quit their current employer "to join a new organization or to do something different." A key reason seems to be their discontent with lack of recognition of and opportunity to develop their talents and skills. Only 28 percent felt their current organization is making full use of the skills they currently have to offer, and 63 percent said their "leadership skills are not being fully developed."[3]

According to Gallup, "The most powerful benefit a manager can provide his or her employees is to place them in jobs that allow them to use the best of their natural talents, adding skills and knowledge to develop and apply their strengths."[4]

Think about the people in your organization. Think about the passion and talent that never catch fire because they never get ignited. Think about the results.

The Voice Conversation is about igniting that fire. It's about unleashing talent to help people make their unique contribution. This is a vital responsibility of leadership. Not only does it impact the job satisfaction, energy, engagement, and nature and quality of an individual's contribution; it also significantly affects the entire culture and the market value of your organization.

The Market Value of Voice

Remember, much of your firm's market value depends on how the market views your people, their combined competence, and how well their competencies match up to customer needs. Research shows that as much as half a firm's market value is based on intangibles such as intellectual capital.[5] And as with any asset, the value of your people depends on how well you leverage them.

In order to make the most of an asset, you need to know all you can about it. Most business leaders really don't know their people well at all. They might know what a person's job is, but they don't know the person—and what passion and purpose inside that person are just waiting to be ignited.

How well do you know the people with whom you work? How much do you understand about their goals, their hopes, their dreams, the things that drive them? What do you really know about their talents, competencies, capacities, skills, wisdom, and experience? What do you know about their deepest values—their principles, scruples, sense of justice, fairness, or integrity? How thoroughly have you thought through their potential contribution—what the company is asking them to give compared to what they *could* give and might really be excited to give?

Though people are not assets in the same way buildings or equipment or patents are, we do speak of them in terms of "human resources." You might want to ask yourself, "Am I really taking the time to delve into those resources and find out what undiscovered value might be buried there?" Of course, no one can measure the worth of a human being, but is it possible that your people are worth a lot more to you than you realize?

Unleashing Talent Through Voice Conversations

The Voice Conversation is a powerful tool to unleash the potential of a human being. The Conversation Guide that follows gives insight into what it means to "find your voice" and why it's so vital. (See Figures 2.2 and 2.3.)

As the guide indicates, voice is at the nexus of need ("What does the world want from you?"), passion ("What do you love doing?"), talent ("What do you do best?"), and conscience ("What do you feel you *should* do?"). When people engage in work that taps their talent and fuels their passion— and rises out of a great need in the world they feel conscience-driven to meet—to paraphrase Dr. Covey, "therein lies their voice, their calling, their soul's code."[6]

The Voice Conversation is about these four elements. The desired outcome is twofold: (1) to create a "Contribution Statement" that helps a person connect with his or her own unique talents and passions and with the purposes and goals of the organization, and (2) to create an environment in which voice is nurtured and encouraged on a daily basis.

FIGURE 2.2

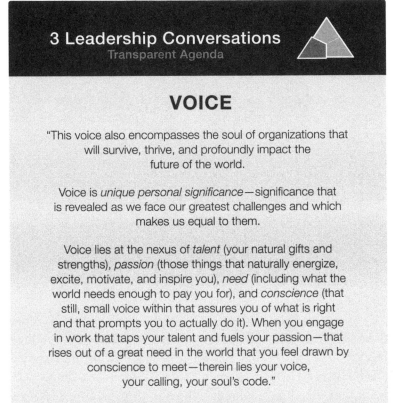

3 Leadership Conversations
Transparent Agenda

VOICE

"This voice also encompasses the soul of organizations that will survive, thrive, and profoundly impact the future of the world.

Voice is *unique personal significance*—significance that is revealed as we face our greatest challenges and which makes us equal to them.

Voice lies at the nexus of *talent* (your natural gifts and strengths), *passion* (those things that naturally energize, excite, motivate, and inspire you), *need* (including what the world needs enough to pay you for), and *conscience* (that still, small voice within that assures you of what is right and that prompts you to actually do it). When you engage in work that taps your talent and fuels your passion—that rises out of a great need in the world that you feel drawn by conscience to meet—therein lies your voice, your calling, your soul's code."

STEPHEN R. COVEY, *THE 8TH HABIT*

FIGURE 2.3

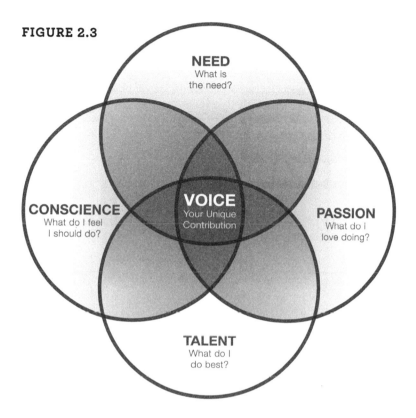

Let's look at each of these four elements in depth. The Conversation Guide contains the key questions you can ask. Other questions that may be helpful to address are also included in this chapter. (See Figure 2.4.)

NEED

1. *What unmet needs and opportunities do you see among our customers, within our business, or in the marketplace?*
2. *What is the ONE thing you could do to make the greatest contribution?*

FIGURE 2.4

3 Leadership Conversations
Transparent Agenda

VOICE

How to Use: Ask each question and then add your perspective—or use your answers to the questions to generate a conversation with the other person.

1. NEED (external or internal)
   a. What unmet needs and opportunities do you see among our customers, within our business, or in the marketplace?
   b. What is the ONE thing you could do to make the greatest contribution?

2. PASSION
   a. What have you always loved doing?
   b. What job or career-related opportunities are you most excited about?

3. TALENT
   a. What are your interests, talents, and capabilities and how could you develop them further?
   b. What could you do well that you're not currently doing?

4. CONSCIENCE
   a. What values or principles are most important to you?
   b. What part of your work do you feel best about, and what would make it more meaningful?

An individual may have great talent, passion, and a positive desire, but unless he or she can apply it to a customer need, it can't be fully unleashed in the organization. As with a broken electrical circuit, a person can generate lots of power, but it won't go anywhere.

So as you have the Voice Conversation, consider together:

- ▶ Who is the customer or key stakeholder?
- ▶ Do others need what this person can contribute enough to pay for it?
- ▶ What is the mission-driven need or opportunity?
- ▶ What is the significance of performing this task or achieving this goal?
- ▶ What is the value of doing it?
- ▶ Is there a big gap that needs to be closed or an opportunity that needs to be achieved?
- ▶ What is the cost or lost value of not doing this?

Of course, fulfilling needs doesn't necessarily bring big money or profit. Public service focuses on contributing to a worthwhile mission. Humanitarian service is a worthy place to invest passions and talents, and the greatest rewards it brings are not monetary. But in a for-profit business, there must be a customer who is willing to pay for a person's talent and contribution.

When you discuss the "one thing" a person could do to make the greatest contribution, keep in mind that at the beginning of the Voice Conversation, neither you nor the person you're leading may have the perspective to accurately make that determination. It may well be a matter of discovery.

Consider the experience of Steve, a star salesperson in his company, and Kelly, his direct manager. Steve was young, but that didn't deter him. He was often the first person in the office, the last to leave, and his success had put him on an exciting career trajectory. He was determined and persistent, but he was also humble and not the type of person to draw overt attention to himself. Kelly, his direct manager, was very pleased with him, often commenting that she wished every employee on her team were like Steve. Steve loved his role. He hadn't expected to go into sales, but it had become intoxicating to him.

> The great servant leaders maintain a sense of humility. They sacrifice their pride and share their power—and their influence both inside and outside their companies is multiplied because of it. Sadly, many people want "spirituality," or at least the appearance of it, without incurring any sacrifice or performing any service.
>
> —STEPHEN R. COVEY

Steve's and Kelly's organization was in high-growth mode, which resulted in a seemingly never-ending need for new talent. After using outsourced recruiters for years, the company ultimately determined to develop a recruiting capability in-house. This, of course, is a specialized skill, and there were no experienced resources available in-house. Then Steve's name came up. He didn't have a background in recruiting, and if he were to shift to this new role, it would leave a large hole on the Sales team. Besides, Steve loved his current role. A shift to this new assignment would mean starting over, with no guarantee of success.

So Kelly and Steve held a Voice Conversation. They discussed Steve's short-term success and his long-term goals. They discussed his talents and his vision for his career. Kelly learned that Steve actually enjoyed a little uncertainty in his life. His ultimate goal was not necessarily to become the CEO one day, but rather to build something meaningful.

He'd had different employment options when he joined this organization, and he chose his employer very deliberately. Consequentially, he felt a significant level of ownership and buy-in to the company mission.

The conversation made it clear to both Steve and Kelly (who would be losing a top salesperson) that Steve's highest contribution to the company would be in building a recruiting function.

While Steve's sales quota had to be filled by someone else, over the subsequent years Steve was responsible for recruiting and hiring hundreds of employees whose success and contribution is attributable, at least in part, to Steve. His Voice Conversation with Kelly became a moment of tremendous leverage for his company.

PASSION

1. *What have you always loved doing?*
2. *What job or career-related opportunities are you most excited about?*

Like most words, "passion" carries different meanings when used in different contexts. In the list of synonyms, words such as "excitement" and "enthusiasm" carry much of the meaning of passion as an element of voice. It grows out of the heart—what a person really cares about, what he or she feels strongly about.

When you conduct a Voice Conversation, make sure to ask "why" when a person reveals his or her enthusiasm.

A team member might say, "I love to run."

"Why do you love to run?"

- ▶ "Because of how it makes me feel."
- ▶ "Because it clears my mind."
- ▶ "Because it gives me time alone."

Another person might say, "I love to create, to invent, to innovate."

"Why do you love to innovate?"

- ▸ "Because of the energy I feel when I create with others."
- ▸ "Because of the thrill I feel when my vision or idea becomes reality."
- ▸ "Because I feel like I'm helping make the world a little better."

Sometimes the reasons are many and varied. Sometimes the answer is "just because." As Steve Jobs said, "You have to follow your heart and your vision. The only way to do great work is to love what you do."[7]

When we seek to find what people care about, it not only helps us help them connect their talents and passion to their work; it also helps us care more deeply about those we lead. Sometimes it's more difficult to care about something or someone we don't understand.

When we do care about people, it's natural to want to help them connect their passion to their work. Many people never make this connection. They often share feelings such as this:

> I never have really understood people who say they love their job. In my mind, I think what they really mean is that this job is better than other jobs, so they "love" it. Or maybe they must not have a life; if all they have is work, they must not have anything else. At any rate, I have never really connected with the idea that I could love my work. It has always been something I *have* to get done so I can do what I really *want* to do.

People who feel like this have not found their voice. As their words reflect, they see work as something that is disconnected from what they *want* to do.

Of course, we can't always connect what excites us to the task in front of us. Still, a thoughtful leader, coach, or mentor can help people create connections. One way to do that is to connect a market *need* that's already been identified to a person's passion.

Consider the experience of Wafa Makhlouf Sayadi, who grew up in love with the magnificent Mediterranean beaches of her native Tunisia. After college, she got a job working in the environmental-services sector, but it wasn't enough for her. She knew she hadn't found her voice. Then one day she volunteered with a group of young people to help clean a beach near the capital city, Tunis.

Sayadi found garbage everywhere. "Food scraps. Refrigerators. Stoves. Dead animals. Fishermen's nets." Totally appalled, she made a sudden connection between her business training and her passion for the spectacular beach. Today she has her own business contracting with municipalities around the Mediterranean to keep the sand clean and the water inviting. Machines do the cleaning, unveiling an immaculate sight that Sayadi relishes. "Sometimes when I get to my home late at night," she says, "I watch the machine going by. It's really heartwarming."[8] Sayadi was able to find her voice by connecting a serious need with a passion that "warms her heart."[9]

Connecting with conscience can also help identify a passion. Many find great energy in what they feel is "the right

> An overwhelming number of people don't write in with specific questions about how to improve their career trajectory. Instead, they write in sharing how they are unhappy—unable to find fulfillment in work and at a loss for what to do to resolve this.
>
> —MAYNARD WEBB

thing to do." By focusing on a job they strongly feel should be done, they realize *that* job can meet an important need.

There are some who suggest people simply "follow their passion"—in other words, if they find something they love, they should just go with it. Encouraging people to do this can be effective, but only to the degree that we understand the whole person and the synergy among the elements of voice. If people follow a path that fails to meet the needs of others, to leverage their talents, or to align with their deep sense of what is right, passion can burn them up instead of firing them up.

As a leader, you will never be as effective as you could be if you don't find your passion and help others find theirs. It's important to understand that the process of discovering passion is generally not instantaneous, but incremental—step by step, conversation by conversation. We change and grow. New passions manifest themselves over time. A great leadership quality to engage in unleashing passion is patience.

TALENT

1. *What are your interests, talents, and capabilities and how could you develop them further?*
2. *What could you do well that you're not currently doing?*

Talent is not only natural or developed ability; it is also a helpful lens through which leaders can look at those they lead. In a way, people are bundles of talents. Everyone has talents. Do you see them in others? Do you see them in yourself?

We often think of talent as something only child prodigies, amazing athletes, or famous celebrities possess. Certainly, there is no question that some people have unusual abilities. But even for those people, the research shows that passion and deliberate practice—and often nurturing from

> Talent is an accident of genes—and a responsibility.
>
> —ALAN RICKMAN

others—contribute as much as their native talent in producing high performance.

Wolfgang Amadeus Mozart had an obvious and celebrated talent for composing music. At the age of 5—competent on both piano and violin—he was already composing. Before his death at the age of 35, he had written more than 600 works, many of which were recognized as masterpieces and have become enduring classics.

Was that an inborn gift, or was it the result of his father's teaching and nurturing combined with many years of disciplined, deliberate practice—and an intense passion for music? A study of his life shows that it was the result of all of these things. True, Mozart had an amazing gift. But he also had a father who recognized that gift at an early age, who discovered the passion of his own voice in nurturing his son's gift, and who sacrificed his own musical career to help Mozart find his voice. In addition, Mozart—impassioned by music—developed his voice by devoting many hours to perfecting his talents through composing, practicing, acquainting himself with the works of other composers, traveling, and performing.

We have learned a lot about how unusual performance is developed and what motivates people to pay the price to develop it—or to help others develop it. Many long-held beliefs about talent have been modified. And the quest to better understand the creation, development, and application of talent continues.

Journalist and researcher Malcolm Gladwell documents this change in the way people look at talent:

For almost a generation, psychologists around the world have been engaged in a spirited debate over a question that most of us would consider to have been settled years ago.

The question is this: is there such a thing as innate talent? The obvious answer is yes. Achievement is talent plus preparation. The problem with this view is that the closer psychologists look at the careers of the gifted, the smaller the role innate talent seems to play and the bigger role preparation seems to play.[10]

So science is moving toward the view that a talent itself is less important than the effort put into the cultivation of the talent. Our purpose is not to convince you that this is true, for we find that most people at some level believe it. Our purpose is to help you become more acutely aware of that belief and of the power of integrating it into the way you think about yourself and others and interact with them as a leader.

According to Gladwell, the job of a leader is to engage in "concerted cultivation"—actively assessing and fostering talent.[11] Busy leaders tend to be shortsighted. They hire talent and then hope it will grow on its own. But this is not effective leadership; it's abdication.

At Google, leadership takes talent development extremely seriously. It's an ongoing conversation throughout the company—a conversation continually stimulated by provocative questions like this: "What if all our engineers were able to reach their potential for innovation?"

Google goes on a serious hunt for answers to questions such as this. They use analytics to measure variances in how their engineers perform. They're not looking for weaknesses;

> You know you have found your life mission when you say, "I dare you to try and take this away from me."
>
> –SHANNON L. ALDER

38

they're looking for strengths. Even small variances can be significant clues to abilities that don't appear on the surface. Then they work at leveraging those abilities.[12]

You don't have to create a People Analytics Department like Google to unleash the talent of those you lead. Voice Conversations asking questions such as the following can go a long way toward accomplishing the same purpose.

- ▶ "What would happen if you were able to reach your full potential in your job?"
- ▶ "How would your work change if you were able to use your talent in some other area?"
- ▶ "Which of your talents are we *not* taking advantage of?"
- ▶ "Which of your talents would you like to grow and develop?"
- ▶ "How would your job change if we matched it better to your talents?"
- ▶ "How do you think we could do that?"

You can also unleash talent by changing what you notice. Watch and listen for hints and clues that a team member might be talented in some area. Then hold a Voice Conversation on that subject. The dividends of such conversations can be significant.

Consider some of the many reality TV programs where people show off their talents. Of course, many competitors have been honing their talents for years. But often those competitors who engage us the most are the ones who seem to just walk in from nowhere.

You might be familiar with the story of Paul Potts, the cellphone salesman who rocked the world in 2007 with his performance of Giacomo Puccini's *Nessun Dorma* as his audition for the first season of the television show *Britain's Got*

Talent. When the 36-year-old, clearly nervous Potts appeared onstage, both judges and audience appeared disinterested and bored. But when he opened his mouth to sing, suddenly jaws dropped, tears were shed, and Potts received a standing ovation. He went on to win the competition and begin a professional musical career, and the video of his audition became one of the most watched videos in YouTube history.

No one would have ever guessed that such talent lay hidden within the meek cellphone salesman. Though Potts had performed in a few amateur productions earlier in his life, he had not even sung in years prior to his audition due to complications from a bike accident. Had he not been given the opportunity to demonstrate his talent, the world would now be without the magnificent contribution of a world-class performer.

Sometimes it takes a "leap of faith" for a person to jump into a role that will more fully engage his or her highest talents. Take Marlene, for example, who worked for a large company. She was always a solid performer. She was the type of employee who could take an assignment, and in a matter of hours, deliver on it in superb ways. However, she was the only employee of her company in her state. As a result of her geographic isolation, her remarkable talents often went unnoticed. If the senior management team had been asked, they would have remarked that she was talented, but truthfully, they may not even have noticed if she had left the company. Her remarkable talents were simply out of sight, out of mind.

A strategic shift in the organization, however, created the opportunity for change for Marlene. The senior leaders had identified a critical company goal, and because of its importance, several roles within the company were reconsidered. Marlene's boss, Brett, held a Voice Conversation with her to determine her interest in shifting from her existing assignment to a role that contributed directly to this new goal.

As they talked together, Marlene realized that the new job would require her to leave a familiar and stable assignment and move to one that put her in a position of risk and uncertainty (as often accompanies major organizational-change efforts), and that it would put her in daily coordination with the company's CEO. If she succeeded, it would have a seismic impact on her organization's strategy and also serve as a catalyst for her career growth. If she failed, her failure would be both public and painful. She also realized that the new assignment aligned with her talents and capabilities in remarkable ways, so she decided to take the leap.

Marlene flourished in this new role. Her many gifts became evident, and she directly contributed to a difficult but ultimately highly successful organizational transformation.

As a leader, your job is to seek out, notice, recognize, encourage, cultivate, and provide opportunities for people to use their talents in ways that will benefit to the max those your organization serves. The mindset of a mediocre leader is, "I need to constantly micromanage and motivate my people to get results." The mindset of a great leader is, "My job is to release the talent and passion of our team toward our highest purposes." The mediocre leader seeks to control; the great leader unleashes talent.

CONSCIENCE

1. *What values or principles are most important to you?*
2. *What part of your work do you feel best about, and what would make it more meaningful?*

The human conscience is one of the most widely validated concepts in psychological, sociological, religious, and philosophical literature throughout time. Conscience is like a moral compass that points the way to choices that are in harmony with natural law and bring the most positive long-term results. We are free to take direction from that compass—or not.

People talk about conscience in different ways, such as an "inner guide," "inner wisdom," or an "inner voice." Most of us remember Jiminy Cricket—the character representing conscience in Walt Disney's film of the Carlo Collodi children's story *Pinocchio*. However we may refer to it, most everyone experiences some kind of deep, quiet, guiding inner sense— and life works better when we pay attention to it.

Acknowledging the voice of conscience is a major element of the FranklinCovey "Voice Finder" process. As leaders, we need to value and listen to the expression of conscience in the people we lead, not just because we don't want to violate their scruples, but also because the way a person responds to conscience can be a key motivator—or demotivator—of productivity.

Harvard Business School Professor John Kotter analyzed 175 companies across 20 industries and found the following results were gained by those leaders and organizations that were willing to solicit feedback from customers, key stakeholders, and employees; that were willing to identify their values and a clear purpose; that were willing to take a stand for their values; and that sought to set an example in the marketplace:

- Leadership focus and time management improved.
- Revenues increased 4 times faster.
- Job creation was 7 times greater.
- Stock price grew 12 times faster.
- Profit performance was 750 percent higher on average.

AUTHOR NOTE Several years ago I spent some significant time working with many of the senior leaders at Procter & Gamble, one of the world's most admired companies. On one occasion during dinner, several people shared with me some of the history of the organization and the core values that had influenced the company culture. They observed that their core values had had a huge impact on their success. They said, "People will often ask each other, 'What is the right thing to do?'" That question seemed to significantly influence many of the choices and decisions that were made.

Because conscience is sometimes easy to ignore, it's a good idea to have frequent "conscience conversations" and audit the values of the team. Ask, "To what degree do we live our values?" Then openly share the results. Values that are not discussed in the open and audited for alignment rarely have much influence.

It's also important to keep in mind that organizations do not have a conscience; only people do. When individuals abdicate conscience, the organization becomes amoral and at serious risk.

Organizations that don't help people connect purpose with individual conscience put their strategic, financial, and cultural values—as well as their unique contribution—at risk. Conscience questions are important in helping those you lead find their voice:

- ▶ "How do you feel about the values and principles of this company?"
- ▶ "Do you feel like we live up to them?"
- ▶ "What principles are most important to you?"
- ▶ "Where are we at risk of being less than true to our principles?"
- ▶ "What does your conscience tell you should be your contribution here?"

In the end, all of these questions add up to, "What do you feel you should do?" Some conscience questions may connect directly back to need:

- ▶ "What do you really feel you should be doing for your customers?"
- ▶ "Where do you feel you may be falling short?"
- ▶ "When might a customer feel that you haven't been straight, or may even have betrayed him or her?"

Other conscience questions may connect back to passion and talent:

- ▶ "What do you feel you should you do with the talents you have?"
- ▶ "What do you feel you should you do with your energy and passion?"

Of course, the conscience connection all begins with us as leaders. Only as we ourselves are in tune with our own conscience and good intent can we effectively talk with others about their connection with theirs. As we create our own conscience connection, we release more of our own talent and passion and become better as leaders, mentors, and coaches in all our leadership roles.

Conscience-connected leaders typically:

- ▶ Have a "people"—not "things"—paradigm. They do not think of people as interchangeable "things," but as unique individuals of infinite worth.
- ▶ Prioritize other people's needs. They constantly assess whether team members are growing healthier, wiser, freer, more autonomous, more capable, and more likely to become leaders in their own right. People do not voluntarily follow self-serving leaders whose goals are to enrich only themselves; they want to follow leaders who place others' interests above their own.[13]

▶ Don't violate their own conscience. Not many of us do this consciously, but leaders who are too busy dealing with crises and have little time for people often make quick, easy, and sometimes less-than-honest choices throughout the day. Those they lead tend to look at their bosses with distrust, not as sources of help.

> Conscience transforms passion into compassion. It engenders sincere caring for others; a combination of both sympathy and empathy, where one's pain is shared and received. Compassion is the interdependent expression of passion.
>
> —STEPHEN R. COVEY

According to *Forbes*, more than 80 percent of workers do not trust their managers to be truthful with them.[14]

▶ Don't obsess over self. Ego is about our own survival, pleasure, and enhancement to the exclusion of others. Ego is selfishly ambitious. It sees relationships in terms of threat or no threat—like little children who classify everybody as either "mean" or "nice." Conscience, on the other hand, democratizes, elevates, and transforms ego to a larger sense of the group, the community, the whole, and the greater good. Conscience sees life in terms of service and contribution, of creating widespread human security and fulfillment.

The way we learn from conscience is through quiet listening and from recognizing feelings and impressions. As we become more sensitive to our own conscience, it leads us to make choices based on deep values and long-range purposes rather than on superficial impulses and shortsighted ambitions. We help others strengthen their conscience connection through searching, thoughtful Voice Conversations.

How Voice Conversations Demonstrate Caring

A leader engaging in Voice Conversations communicates deep, genuine caring. It says to a person, "I value you. I value your feelings about what is important. I value your unique talents and strengths. I want to help you discover and explore them so that together we can design your job to enable you to make your greatest possible contribution and help our team succeed."

As you engage in caring Voice Conversations, you unleash personal talent and potential, which not only brings great joy and personal satisfaction to followers, but also significantly increases both the quantity and quality of human resources available to the organization.

As with each of the 3 Leadership Conversations, the Voice Conversation is not just a one-time event, but an ongoing dialogue. One man shared his experience with a leader who helped him find his voice through many Voice Conversations:

> I had been a schoolteacher for about 12 years when I decided to give it up. I loved teaching, but the pay was terrible and the school was a discouraging place. I felt nobody valued what I was doing, so I figured why not try something else? Then my sister-in-law introduced me to her friend Richard, a prominent man in our community who owned an important business-consulting company.
>
> Richard started asking me questions. What had I done in my life? What did I like to do? What was my family like? He seemed to show real interest in me, which surprised and intrigued me. Then he invited me to do a project for him. I

knew he was trying me out to see what I could do, but I really enjoyed the project. It scared me—I'd never done anything like it—but my training and education was just right for it.

At one point he asked me to do a project that was a little beyond my scope. I probably had built up a little too much confidence, and it fell apart on me. I took a lot of criticism from both the customer and my colleagues, and I was discouraged. But in front of everyone, Richard said, "Wait a minute. Let's think this through." He took me aside and we had several talks over the following weeks. He didn't discuss my blunders. Instead we talked about what I had learned and, once again, how my vision of my future had changed. Then we talked about stuff we had been reading. We talked about my passion for music and his passion for fishing. As I look back on it, I realize that Richard was not "tutoring" or doing a "human-resources-management thing" on me—he was genuinely interested in me as a human being.

Richard's confidence in me paid off. I became so good at my job that customers would ask for me personally when they needed training. Eventually, he challenged me again by giving me a leadership role in the company. Again I was scared—I had never been educated to be a business manager. But he kept calling me in for talks, asking me what I thought we should do, and listening as if I were some great business consultant. It stretched me mentally and emotionally. For some reason, he put much value on my thoughts and feelings and aspirations. These conversations molded me into an effective business leader as I found myself modeling him in helping other consultants grow and develop.

When I think about it, no leader I'd ever had—and I had taught in schools led by a number of principals—had ever shown any interest in me at all. Richard was not only the best boss I ever had, but he was also a great friend and teacher, mostly by example.

Because of this ongoing human connection, Richard helped this man find his voice—that link among need, passion, talent, and conscience that enabled him to make a significant positive contribution. He unleashed talent that otherwise would have remained dormant in a man whose contribution would otherwise likely have only been mediocre.

Another way the Voice Conversation demonstrates caring—and differs from other "talent management" approaches—is how the conversation addresses the whole person: body, heart, mind, and spirit. Most other approaches center almost exclusively on career goals, a focus more suited to Performance Conversations. Questions in a Voice Conversation, by contrast, appropriately address all four needs of the whole person.

Below are some examples of questions you might ask in each area.

LIFE PURPOSE AND MEANING

- ▶ "What do you find meaningful in your work?"
- ▶ "How do you think it could be more fulfilling?"
- ▶ "How do you feel about the contribution we're making as a team?"
- ▶ "What do you think we could we do to improve that contribution?"

INTELLECTUAL GROWTH AND SKILL DEVELOPMENT

- ▶ "What have you been learning lately?"
- ▶ "What do you enjoy reading?"
- ▶ "What lessons could you share with the rest of us?"
- ▶ "Are you getting the skill training and development you need?"
- ▶ "What skills do you feel you could you teach others?"

SOCIAL/EMOTIONAL ISSUES

> For the person with creative potential there is no wholeness except in using it.
>
> —ROBERT K. GREENLEAF

- ▶ "How are you getting along with the team?"
- ▶ "How can you best empower and fully engage your team members?"
- ▶ "Have you been able to establish some helpful friendships here at work?"
- ▶ "What do you think we could do to improve the culture and spirit of the team?"
- ▶ "What do you feel you could you do to help the team work better?"

PHYSICAL HEALTH AND FINANCIAL WELL-BEING

- ▶ "How is your health?"
- ▶ "Are you managing to effectively balance work and life?"
- ▶ "What areas of your health and wellness would you like to improve?"
- ▶ "Are you doing all right financially?"
- ▶ "Are you meeting your financial goals?"

We encourage you to consider asking questions like these about the four needs and making mutual commitments with those you lead to answer them. The more you satisfy these needs, the more you demonstrate caring and the more talent you can unleash—and retain.

Professor Greg Unruh at George Mason University tells of one "high-potential" leader, a former MBA student who was fast-tracked in his company and looked to be well on his way to great things. Then he suddenly quit. When asked why, he said, "I was only using a tenth of my *being* at work."

As we have worked with leaders throughout the world, we have discovered that many of them are still stuck in an Industrial Age mindset, thinking of people as interchangeable parts—as "things" to be managed. One of our first tasks is to help these leaders understand that in our Knowledge Age, a leader's job is to unleash talent, passion, and contribution, and only as a leader addresses the "whole person" can he or she do this most effectively.

Creating a Contribution Statement

So, what is the desired outcome of a Voice Conversation?

When people find their voice, they get clear on the most significant contribution they can make—right at the nexus of need, passion, talent, and conscience. A formal Voice Conversation should lead to a *definition* of that contribution. We call this a "Contribution Statement."

Below are some examples of Contribution Statements:

▶ *My contribution is to make sure every hydraulic part we ship is top quality. When I come to work, I see in my mind's eye the mothers and fathers and children who fly on our airplanes, and I can't afford to be less than totally alert to any problems with the parts. For me, it's my number-one responsibility.* —Sev, quality inspector, airplane manufacturing company

▶ *[My contribution is] to use my creativity and positivity to improve my clients' whole environment. I'm not just another property agent. I'm excited to find out what unique needs and interests they have so I can build exactly the kind of home that will give them the best kind of life.* —Yoli, real estate agent

▶ *I keep people happy by keeping hot fries hot and nobody ever has to ask me for refills. It's a game I win every day, and I love it.* —Bunter, server, fast-food restaurant

> Each of us is a unique strand in the intricate web of life and here to make a contribution.
>
> –DEEPAK CHOPRA

▶ *I combine my passion for design with the customer's need for edgy ways to distinguish themselves in the marketplace. I can't settle for anything less than a design that's categorically different from anything else that's out there.* —Peter, graphic designer

What difference would it make to your organization if everyone on your team had a Contribution Statement? Would they be clearer about their own purpose at work? Would they be more excited about that purpose? Would they see more value in it? Would they feel that their talents were better being used? Would they feel more like they had found their voice?

And what about you? What would be the payoff if you had your own Contribution Statement?

The Leadership Rewards of Helping People Find Their Voice

The process of helping individuals find their voice communicates that both the organization and the leader care about people and value what they can offer. It communicates the benefits of harnessing others' capacity for the good of all. It clarifies and communicates the role of a leader to recognize, unleash, and orchestrate human capacity rather than to simply manage and control people.

It also magnifies the leader in the process. Take a moment and reflect on your own experience. If you have ever worked to help others find their voice, have you learned more about your own abilities to contribute?

> **AUTHOR NOTE** One of my first assignments as a manager was to head up the Training and Development department in a service organization. As I stepped into the role, I found I had inherited an assistant named Kathy. In a conversation with her, I discovered that she had a master's degree in English and loved to write. The only reason she was in her current position was because it was all that was available at the time.
>
> As part of my job, I needed to write a number of letters, which took a great deal of my time. It occurred to me that if I were to ask Kathy to write preliminary drafts, we might be able to get things done better and faster. She was happy to accept that assignment, and she did an amazing job. In fact, I found that I could tell her what was needed, and she would write the communication more clearly and succinctly than I could ever have done—and far more quickly. All I had to do was review it (usually few, if any, changes needed to be made) and then sign it. As a result, we were able to do more, and better, in less time.
>
> As my confidence in Kathy's abilities grew, I quickly realized she might have more to offer in helping to create training materials. Again, I found that once she understood what was needed, she was so good at capturing and organizing ideas and writing them clearly that even her initial efforts took projects far beyond the "rough draft" stage. It wasn't long before my "assistant" became my "lead writer" and received the accompanying raise in pay.
>
> During this process, several things became very clear to me. First, Kathy was really enjoying this new dimension of her work. She had been in the job for months, and her talents had never been fully utilized. But with these new responsibilities, she was finding real satisfaction in being able to contribute in ways that more fully engaged her talents. She eventually went on to receive other promotions.
>
> Second, by helping Kathy use more of her talents on the job, I was able to better recognize and focus on using my own talents. While I was good at identifying needs and desired results and the process of getting there, she

> was good at capturing, organizing, and giving verbal expression to those things. As we were both "unleashed" to work in our areas of strength, we were much more effective as partners.
>
> The third insight came much later. As I moved on to other leadership roles, I found I was much more attuned to look for talents and abilities that were right in front of me but unrecognized. This made me a better leader in all my leadership roles moving forward.

On the organizational level, at the nexus of need, passion, talent, and conscience, a top-performing organization has, in effect, found its "organizational voice." This happens when the people on all levels in the organization are good at what they do and love doing it. They feel what they do is valuable. It's how they make their unique contribution. And both their leaders and customers love what they do and how they do it.

That's when an organization sparks that inner synergy and fire that marks a world-class team.

Creating an Environment of Voice Conversation

While a *formal* Voice Conversation results in a Contribution Statement that connects a person with his or her own voice and the important goals of the organization, *informal* Voice Conversations create the *environment* that consistently nurtures and engages voice. And you can initiate an informal Voice Conversation almost anytime.

For example, you might notice that someone has learned a new skill, or a new talent bubbles to the surface. You might say:

> ▶ "I just noticed that you're really good at solving problems. You can break down complex situations and see the simple answer."

53

▶ "I noticed how well you managed that project. You know how to set clear goals; you stayed on task and timelines. You also seem very good with managing on budget."

Or you might notice a sudden burst of excitement from a team member:

▶ "You really got into that discussion about research. I didn't know that was an interest to you."

▶ "I notice that when new people join the team, you take a real interest in them. You make it a lot easier for them to adapt to the rest of us."

Or you might just give a word of voice encouragement.

AUTHOR NOTE Early in my career, a colleague and I were asked to open our company's first field office, about 2,000 miles away. I was expected to represent my organization to high-level government officials and corporate leaders. Grateful for the job and eager for the opportunity, I was still apprehensive.

Just before I left for the new job, a leader I respected pulled me aside. He knew I was nervous. I told him I'd go out and get great sales leads for him to follow up on. But he stopped me in mid-sentence and spoke very directly. "You're now a senior member of this firm. You won't be getting leads for me—you'll be closing deals yourself. You don't need to rely on me or anyone else. I trust you. I believe in you."

As simple as it was, that short conversation completely changed the way I viewed myself and my capabilities. My expectations of myself rose to the level of his trust in me. Just those few words gave me the confidence to meet the challenge.

Over the years, we've asked our clients to talk about people who have helped them find their voice and believed in them, even when they didn't believe in themselves. They've talked about leaders who entrusted them with jobs bigger than they thought they could handle. They've told stories about wise mentors and coaches they have learned to love. Usually, they say things like this:

- ▶ "This person believed in me."
- ▶ "She saw more in me than I did in myself."
- ▶ "He trusted me, and I didn't want to let him down."
- ▶ "She cared deeply about me, listened to me, and helped me discover more about myself than I ever knew."
- ▶ "He challenged me and gave me the loyalty and support needed to make difficult decisions."
- ▶ "When I made mistakes, he always created a learning environment where we could reflect and talk openly and honestly about how to get better, not punishment or fearful situations where we would avoid or blame others."

There's respect in their voices—almost palpable reverence. Strikingly, almost everyone we talk with can speak of someone who transformed their lives for the better. As author Blaine Lee has observed, those we honor are those who have influenced us the most. Often it is those who believed in us, even when we did not believe in ourselves.[15]

This is the power of the Voice Conversation. It is not some new thing; it is just something that needs to be recognized and expanded. Your influence with others grows as you help them find and engage their voice. And this often happens in your day-to-day conversations with those you lead.

It All Begins With You

So how does it happen? In short, person by person and conversation by conversation. And it all begins with you.

- ▶ *You* are the one who decides to recognize and value a need.
- ▶ *You* are the one who decides to nurture enthusiasm and passion for a path and purpose.

55

- ▶ **You** are the one who decides to seek out, recognize, and foster talent.
- ▶ **You** are the one who decides to harness the power of conscience and conviction among those you lead.

Most critically, *you* are the one who sets the example. The single most important thing you can do as a leader to influence others to find their voice is to find your own. Trying to help others light the fire within when your own fire is sputtering or nonexistent is an exercise in futility. On the other hand, when your voice manifests itself regularly and you have effective Voice Conversations with others, they will catch fire themselves.

> **AUTHOR NOTE** Years ago, Stephen R. Covey and I were discussing a document he had produced sometime earlier that had had a profound influence on me. He shared with me the story of how the content of this document had come about and how he gained a powerful insight into the role of leaders that became foundational not only to the whole idea of Principle-Centered Leadership, the 7 Habits, and all that he worked on throughout his life, but also to my own personal leadership and teaching over the past 50 years.
>
> Stephen said he had been up late one night working on a document to help leaders supervise teachers in an organization. As he was struggling to understand how leaders could best do this, it suddenly came to his awareness that the most important role of a leader is to help followers learn to be responsible for and "govern" themselves, and the most effective way a leader could do that was to (1) teach followers the timeless, universal principles that create positive results; (2) help followers set their own goals to accomplish desired results; then (3) become a source of help to them as they work to accomplish those goals and achieve those results. He said he became so excited about this concept of leadership that he rushed over to his colleague's house early the next morning to share it; then he spent the rest of his life exploring it, developing it, applying it, and teaching it to others.
>
> The document Stephen wrote as a result of his experience had given me great insight into some powerful principles of effective leadership. But more

important, his example and his passion over the years fueled my fire about the importance of discovering my own leadership voice.

When we openly recognize the strengths and talents of those around us and tap into their passions, they see themselves more clearly and are empowered to build on their strengths.

AUTHOR NOTE I have found that my most personally rewarding Voice Conversations happen at home with my children. Every month I sit down and have a one-on-one conversation with each child. We have had these since they were tiny. I sit with them in a quiet room and give them my full, uninterrupted attention so they can feel listened to and feel my interest. I sit with paper and pen and ask them some questions:

- "What's going on in your life that excites you?"
- "How are you using your talents?"
- "How are you helping others—your friends and family members?"
- "What are your future plans?"
- "How do you feel about the ways you are spending your time?"
- "What would you like to do in your life?"

During these conversations, I just listen, and I am motivated and inspired by their willingness to share their dreams, their fears, and their challenges. As their father, I give what guidance and direction I can, or help them think through and solve a problem themselves. Sometimes solutions can be found by simply thinking through things out loud, together.

I also talk about the strengths I see in them. For example:

"Luke, it is really interesting that you have 10 or 20 people wanting to be around you all the time. It's because you're fun. People like being around you. They like your sense of humor. They like your personality. You make people feel comfortable."

"McKay, you are a really good boy. You are always so curious. You are always so kind and considerate and happy and positive. You are quick to forgive and rarely get upset. You are a great example to those around you."

> I make a point of acknowledging these things aloud—these talents and skills they may not even see in themselves. This acknowledgment increases their self-awareness and self-confidence. At one point, one of the boys who didn't even want to talk to me in the first place ended up talking for an hour straight and didn't want me to leave!

Watchouts

With each of the Leadership Conversations, there are certain "watchouts" to be aware of. These deal with attitudes leaders should avoid in conducting these conversations.

Attitude watchouts for Voice Conversations include the following (see Figure 2.5):

- ▶ "This 'voice' stuff is irrelevant; my job is to make sure people do their job."
- ▶ "We talk about people's potential in their annual performance review."
- ▶ "I'll do this if I have time."
- ▶ "Who cares if people are fired up as long as they're doing the job they were hired to do?"
- ▶ "I assume people will naturally trust me enough to share what's important to them."
- ▶ "I already know what's important to others."
- ▶ "As long as we're making money, what does it matter?"

Attitudes and beliefs such as these defeat the very purpose of the Voice Conversation. They are the assumptions of a manager of things, not a leader of people.

You might want to take a minute now to honestly examine your own beliefs. Do any of the assumptions on the guide describe the way you think or feel? If so, you might want to think about the impact of these attitudes and reconsider your approach.

FIGURE 2.5

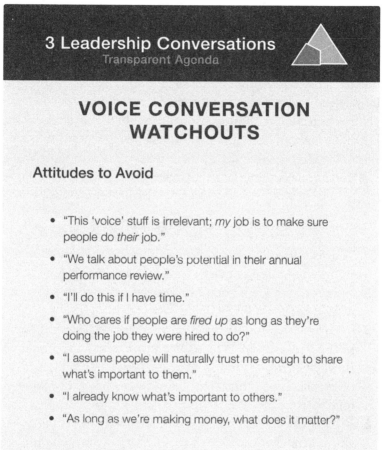

3 Leadership Conversations
Transparent Agenda

VOICE CONVERSATION WATCHOUTS

Attitudes to Avoid

- "This 'voice' stuff is irrelevant; *my* job is to make sure people do *their* job."
- "We talk about people's potential in their annual performance review."
- "I'll do this if I have time."
- "Who cares if people are *fired up* as long as they're doing the job they were hired to do?"
- "I assume people will naturally trust me enough to share what's important to them."
- "I already know what's important to others."
- "As long as we're making money, what does it matter?"

Only as you recognize the value of each member of your team, as you genuinely care about helping team members discover their unique talents and passions, and as you work to help them find the place where they can best and most happily contribute will you be able to fully tap into the talents, energy, commitment, and synergy that lead to top performance.

A Final Thought

Voice gives context to work, and context gives meaning. Yes, we must do our work and do it well in order to keep a job and succeed. But when we see that work in the context of meeting a real need that is important and that we really care about, and we have and are developing talents that significantly contribute to the accomplishment of the work, the work becomes *meaningful*. This is the path from survival to greatness. Getting ourselves and others on the path through Voice Conversations is the opportunity of great leadership.

DISCUSSION QUESTIONS

1. Why is a Voice Conversation an ongoing conversation rather than a single event?
2. What can you do if you find no need in a person's job for what he or she does well and loves to do?
3. Who are the people with whom you feel you should be holding meaningful Voice Conversations?
4. In what ways does it make a difference when people bring passion to their work? How can you tell if people love their work?
5. Why is sincere listening so critical to a Voice Conversation? In what ways can Voice Conversations change relationships?
6. Do the people in your organization have latent talents and abilities that are not being used? What if the person you converse with has no desire to bring passion or talent to the job?
7. What is your own unique contribution? How would you describe your voice?

CHAPTER 3

THE PERFORMANCE CONVERSATION

At the highest level, the work of a leader is to lead conversations about what is essential and what is not.

—RONALD A. HEIFETZ, *Leadership Without Easy Answers*

AUTHOR NOTE Early in my career, I had a great boss who also served as my business coach. This man led a division of about 20 people. We would all meet together each Monday morning and review our mission, strategy, and account pipeline. We were focused on performance and living our mission and values. We all cared deeply about hitting our goals and financial targets, but our individual and team focus was far beyond that. We had a deep sense that we were truly making a difference in the lives of those we served. We would consistently share stories of how our efforts had impacted people's lives.

The team operated in a very high level of synergy. Everyone on the team was a top performer and sought to live up to the mission. Each of us knew exactly how our role contributed to the overall strategy and performance of the team, and no one wanted to let anybody down. The culture and spirit of the team was fun, unified, and even family-like. We all felt that everyone on the team could be trusted and had a unique contribution to make.

My boss met regularly with each team member, one-on-one, to review our performance agreements. These agreements contained clear desired results, including goals, measures, and timelines. After we reviewed our agreements, we would make updates or modifications if needed. These agreements were a key part of building and sustaining relationships of high trust. I knew my boss and all of the other team members were mutually dedicated to being resources to me and to each other. I knew they were there to provide me with guidance, coaching, and support as needed. My boss consistently built trust with me through his continual demonstrations that I mattered to him and that he had confidence in me. He extended high levels of trust and responsibility to me in instances where I was probably too young or too junior for the high-profile assignment. He continually demonstrated that I mattered to him, that he could trust me, and that my performance was important to all of us.

This was one of the best times in my career. For three years in a row, we were consistently the number-one division in our company in revenue and profitability. I attribute our team success and motivation to my boss's superb leadership direction and support. Early on in my career, he became a great mentor and role model I wanted to emulate.

Have you ever been part of a high-performance team—a team of people who were all capable, eager, excited, and contributing; a team that really did accomplish great things? If so, do you often think about or even relate to the story of that team? Do you remember it as one of the best times of your life?

How did you feel about the leader's support, loyalty, and advocacy on your behalf? What happened when everyone was very clear on the vision and desired outcomes? Did everyone dig deeply for hidden inner resources? Were you closely following the score or measure of success? Did you relish the wins that came?

There are all kinds of great teams, including athletic teams, service clubs, debate teams, work teams, and others. But they all have at least one thing in common: an unusually high level of performance and accomplishment.

Management expert Howard M. Guttman defines a high-performing team this way:

> A high-performing team is a fully aligned entity that operates horizontally to achieve increasingly higher levels of results. There is fundamental agreement on the business strategy. Roles are clear and accountability is redefined to include peers holding one another—and the leader—accountable for results. Protocols are in place for decision making, conflict management, and team behavior.
>
> Relationships are transparent and avoid silo defensiveness. There is an unmistakable "we"-ness to how a high-performing team conducts itself.[1]

In simpler terms, members of high-performing teams know exactly what the goal is, what their roles are, how they keep score, how they make decisions, and how to get through conflicts—and they're getting better at doing these things all the time. In high-performing teams, it's never about "me"; it's about "we."

In his landmark book *The Fifth Discipline*, systems scientist Peter M. Senge describes the engaging nature of a great team:

> When you ask people about what it is like being part of a great team, what is most striking is the meaningfulness of the experience. People talk about being part of something larger than themselves, of being connected, of being generative. It becomes quite clear that, for many, their experiences as part of truly great teams stand out as singular periods of life lived to the fullest. Some spend the rest of their lives looking for ways to recapture that spirit.[2]

If you want to be a great leader, coach, or mentor, building a high-performing team should be a top priority. Here's why:

▶ *In today's organizations, the rate of change and innovation is too fast for one person to handle.* Great leaders no longer make all the key decisions alone. It's not sustainable. They'd burn out—and while they did last, they would create a dependent culture of "yes" people who would be compliant and mentally lazy, which certainly doesn't unleash the talent necessary to create a high-performance organization. Today's great leaders look laterally at each team member and engage the "voices" of those they lead.

▶ *Technology means top managers don't own information.* Leaders no longer sit at the top of the information hierarchy, and knowledge is no longer their sole property. With knowledge sharing, search engines, and texting, we're all on an equal footing now—which is actually a huge benefit in unleashing talent.

▶ *A more empowered workforce is more engaged and productive.* The Gallup organization recently reported that companies with higher-than-average employee engagement also had 22 percent higher profits, 21 percent higher productivity, and 25 percent lower turnover.[3]

▶ *An empowered workforce is more aligned with an organization's business goals.* The more people understand the goals of the organization—and the freer they feel to engage in finding ways to use their talents and build their skills to meet those goals—the more effectively those goals can be accomplished. High-performance organizations are aligned and streamlined to accomplish with minimal waste.

> When we're fueled by the fear of what other people think or that gremlin that's constantly whispering "You're not good enough" in our ear, it's tough to show up. We end up hustling for our worthiness rather than standing in it.
>
> —BRENÉ BROWN

So why do managers fail to build high-performing teams?

Most often because they lack the mindset and skillset to talk honestly, clearly, and positively about performance—in other words, to hold effective "Performance Conversations." Their mindset is to be "in charge," to hold information close, to worry about who gets credit and whose turf is whose, and to distrust their people precisely because of their fear of failure.

One symbol of this failure is the dreaded "performance review."

Why Traditional "Talent Management" Falls Flat

Traditionally, many organizations have a talent-management system in which people are scheduled to meet with the boss and discuss their "performance"—yearly, twice a year, quarterly, or whenever.

During these meetings, leaders and team members generally put on the table their strategies, Balanced Scorecards, KPIs, or goals statements. Leaders give "feedback" (which is typically negative and sandwiched in between obligatory commendation). Sometimes team members make impressive (but often vague) commitments—but after the meeting, they move on and get swallowed up again in the "real job." Sometimes they remember filling out forms, but they can't quite recall what was on those forms.

Deep down, nearly everyone hates these performance reviews.

According to some experts, performance reviews are a "sham"—sometimes described as "insidious," "damaging," "pretentious," and "bogus." They cause unhealthy competition, pitting team member against team member. They are "neither useful nor effective."[4] They are incredibly biased. In fact, one study showed that nearly two-thirds of a performance rating reflects the rater's biases and has little to do with the person being rated.[5]

At least three major university studies of performance reviews confirm that almost everyone—on both the receiving end and the giving end of performance reviews—really *does* hate these reviews. They tend to "discourage even the best performers and the most industrious employees."[6] According to performance-appraisal expert Kevin Murphy, "Annual reviews end up as a source of anxiety and annoyance rather than a source of useful information."[7]

When you think about it, it's amazing that people go to work every day, do their best, feel incredibly busy and overworked, experience pressure and anxiety, and then go through this bizarre exercise that almost everyone hates. Even more amazing is the fact that they do this even though the whole exercise often turns out to be completely useless. When things actually do go off track, bewildered people start faultfinding and finger-pointing in all directions, with bosses blaming workers for poor performance and workers blaming bosses for poor leadership.

But still, performance reviews are ubiquitous—nearly everyone has to go through them.

The question is: Why? If performance reviews are so universally despised and most people agree they're useless, why do companies continue to hold them? Why is something as essential as worker performance handled so poorly?

We suggest it's because many leaders genuinely don't know of a better alternative.

Talking about performance is necessary. "It should happen every day," says Professor Samuel A. Culbert of the UCLA Anderson School of Management. "But employees need evaluations they can believe, not the fraudulent ones they receive. They need evaluations that are dictated by need, not a date on a calendar. They need evaluations that make them strive to improve, not pretend they are perfect."[8]

Why doesn't this intelligent, timely kind of conversation happen more often? Basically, because many leaders don't know how to do it—and they're very busy doing other things.

In this chapter, we're going to show you how to hold what we call "Performance Conversations." (See Figure 3.1.)

FIGURE 3.1

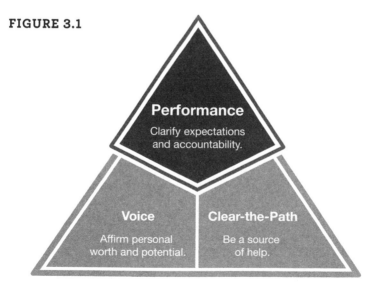

Formal Performance Conversations between leaders and teams or team members result in written agreements that create shared vision and clarity in each of the five vital elements of performance. The spirit of the agreement is to partner *with* people rather than having them work *for* you or *under* you. We often call these "Win-Win Performance Agreements" because they represent a "win" for the individual and a "win" for the organization.

Informal Performance Conversations happen throughout the organization all the time. They enable leaders to constantly reinforce the Win-Win Performance Agreement and address issues immediately, when the impact is small and there's time to do something about it.

Once you understand the difference between traditional performance reviews and Performance Conversations, we're convinced you'll see the same thing we've seen through our experience with companies worldwide: having Performance Conversations—both formal and informal—is far more important than doing many of the "day job" tasks leaders feel are so urgent at the time. In fact, they even eliminate or change the nature of many of these tasks. They also lead to a culture of top performance—of engaged people who combine their "voices" and work in synergy to accomplish amazing results.

The Performance Conversation— *Not* Your Old Performance Review

Performance Conversations are significantly different from typical performance reviews. They allow leaders to "let go of the ego"—to forego their need to be the smartest, the executor, the doer, or the hero and encourage people to work together to co-create and have a shared set of outcomes, objectives, goals, targets, and deliverables.

Consider the power of having clear, shared expectations in these areas. Think about the last time you were frustrated or disappointed with someone's performance—or someone was disappointed with yours. Were the expectations really clear? Or were you operating under a series of assumptions? By effectively putting people on the "same page," Performance Conversations eliminate problems created by mismatched expectations.

These conversations also allow team members to fully engage, because people feel the excitement of determining how they can perform to make their unique contribution. In fact, it's performance in the context of voice (contribution) that gives meaning to performance, unleashes talent, and lights the fire within those who perform.

It would be hard to overemphasize the importance of the relationship between the Voice Conversation and the Performance Conversation. Because the Voice Conversation is about discovering a person's purpose, talents, and desired contribution, it logically comes first, so that in the Performance Conversation, you're talking about how to connect voice with purpose. The Contribution Statement from the Voice Conversation can be an excellent guide to goal setting in the Performance Conversation.

If circumstances are such that you are entering the process "midstream," however, you can tie the elements of voice and performance together as you proceed. For example, in a formal Performance Conversation where you're looking together at the Performance Conversation Guide, you might say something like this:

"Rick, I noticed that when we talk about [a particular project], you seemed to be really excited. Tell me why you feel so strongly about it." After listening carefully, you might say: "That's very interesting. I'd like to talk more about that with you. Let me give you another guide to look at. This is about what's called a Voice Conversation. Can we schedule some time to talk about those things that are most important and engaging to you?" You could make a suggestion like this during an informal Performance Conversation as well.

Unlike performance reviews, Performance Conversations are not infrequently scheduled events to be dreaded; they are rich, ongoing interactions between leaders and team members that both can look forward to, and through which they can discover high performance and immense satisfaction.

Consider some of the key differences between performance reviews and Performance Conversations as listed in Figure 3.2. Let's look at these differences a little more deeply.

Timing. Where the performance review is a rare, scheduled, formal event, Performance Conversations are frequent and are both formal and informal. Formal Performance Conversations are scheduled occasionally to create "big picture" clarity; informal Performance Conversations become a constant way of communicating that happens many times throughout any given day. In Performance Conversations, people deal with real issues as they come up—not six months down the road after they've forgotten what the issues even were.

Orientation. A performance review primarily looks back over six months or a year. The focus is on what happened, not on what could happen. Performance Conversations, on the other hand, are focused on the present and the future. They are what Professor Culbert calls "performance *pre*views" rather than "performance reviews."[9]

Goals. Performance reviews typically leave people with too many goals or goals that are unclear and unmeasurable. Performance Conversations leave workers with clear expectations and goals that are specific, measurable, voice-fulfilling (therefore motivating), and aligned with the goals of the organization. (See Figure 3.3.)

FIGURE 3.2

Performance Reviews	Performance Conversations
Once or twice a year	Often—sometimes even multiple times in a given day
Backward-looking	Forward-looking
Unclear or unrealistic goals	Clear goals based on "voice" that is agreed to and aligned with the goals of the organization
Unclear action steps	Clear action steps to achieve those goals
Negative feedback sandwiched in between obligatory commendation	Positive feedback focused on the future
Outcome: forgotten within a few days	Outcome: specific, measurable, frequently tracked results

FIGURE 3.3

Instead of:	This:
"Focus on quality improvement."	"Earn a green belt in Six Sigma quality control by the end of the quarter."
"Work on people skills."	"Complete all three modules of communication training by May 31."
"Improve sales this next quarter."	"Identify three decision makers from the list of potential Tier 1 clients and develop a service relationship with each of them by December 1."

As leaders engage in ongoing informal Performance Conversations about such goals, the goals remain memorable and motivating. They invite discussion of opportunities and better ways to achieve them.

Action steps. Performance reviews often leave team members without specific action steps to help them reach their goals. In Performance Conversations, people commit to do specific things that will lead to goal achievement. They're held accountable only for things they have control over, and usually for things they themselves have suggested.

Confidence building. Performance reviews typically cover items involving past performance issues—mostly weaknesses—sandwiched in between obligatory words of "positive feedback." Performance Conversations are forward-focused and positive. The conversation is about how to move forward in making a contribution. Goals are created to leverage the person's voice.

Outcomes. Performance reviews are so rare, and the days between so busy, that they're quickly forgotten until the next one looms on the horizon. Goals that were set in the previous review have evaporated in the whirlwind of the day-to-day. Formal Performance Conversations result in Win-Win Performance Agreements that create shared clarity and commitment in the five major elements of performance. In addition, informal Performance Conversations happen all the time. Leaders and team members are constantly communicating about goals and issues. Outcomes are clearly defined and celebrated.

SO, WHAT GOES INTO A PERFORMANCE CONVERSATION?

The purpose of a Performance Conversation is to improve performance by creating an agreement that establishes priority, focuses effort, clarifies process, and develops trust.

These conversations demonstrate a leader's caring in meaningful, measurable ways. They say, "I value clear communication between us regarding your job performance. I want us both to clearly understand what's expected and how results are measured. I want you to have the satisfaction of knowing when your performance is excellent and how it affects the success of the team. I want you to have confidence that if there is a problem with your performance, we can talk it over and search for ways to improve."

In addition to caring about the members of the team, these conversations communicate a leader's caring about the work these people do. That's why the leader is focused on creating a win for both the organization and the individual. This caring is also vital to unleashing the talent of the team. Can you imagine working with a leader in the field of healthcare who didn't really care about the quality of service given to patients? A leader's communication of caring about the work inspires team members to care about the work as well.

In formal Performance Conversations, leaders and team members agree on five things:

1. **Desired Results** (*What* is important and *why.*)
2. **Guidelines** (*How* it is to be accomplished.)
3. **Resources** (*What* the team member has to work with.)
4. **Accountability** (*How* performance can be *tracked* and *improved.*)
5. **Consequences** (*What* constitutes a *win* for everyone.)

The outcome of agreement on these five issues is not only a written Win-Win Performance Agreement; it is also the basis for ongoing informal Performance Conversations. (See Figures 3.4 and 3.5.)

FIGURE 3.4

3 Leadership Conversations
Transparent Agenda

PERFORMANCE

In a well-conducted performance conversation,
the individual worker agrees on **what** is important, **why** it
is important, **how** it is to be accomplished, and how it can
be **tracked and improved**. The worker begins to both
see and share commitment to the overall organizational
vision, mission, strategies, and goals. It is not a one-way
conversation, particularly when the worker is not new on
the job. It is a win-win-win conversation—a win for the
organization, a win for the boss, and a win for the
worker in helping them align and achieve their most
important goals and objectives.

TALENT UNLEASHED

"As a rule there are in everyone all sorts of good ideas,
ready like tinder. But much of this tinder catches fire...only
when it meets some flame or spark...from
some other person."

-ALBERT SCHWEITZER

FIGURE 3.5

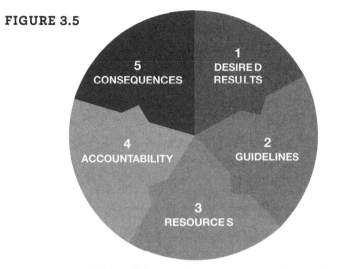

Because all five of these elements are vital to Performance Conversations, we have developed a Conversation Guide for each. In the rest of this chapter, we'll go into "micro" vision and focus on each of these elements; then we'll pull back to "panoramic" vision to look at the Performance Conversation as a whole.

The exciting thing to keep in mind about the Performance Conversation is in Albert Schweitzer's observation: "In everyone's life, at some time, our inner fire goes out. It is then burst into flame by an encounter with another human being. We should all be thankful for those people who rekindle the inner spirit." The Performance Conversation is a wonderful tool for leaders to use to ignite that kind of fire.

Step 1: Desired Results

The number-one job of leaders and managers is to focus effort toward accomplishing desired results. In this part of the Performance Conversation, we drill down to clarify the results teams and individuals want to accomplish, and identify the measurable goals that will lead to achieving those results. (See Figure 3.6.)

Consider asking questions such as these:

1. What are the team's top two or three goals?
2. How will we measure success?
3. What are your top two or three individual goals—the goals you need to achieve in order to make your contribution?
4. How do your individual goals connect to the team's top goals? Why are your goals important?
5. Are your goals realistic and achievable?
6. How have you translated these goals into plans (i.e., who will do what by when)?
7. How will you measure your success?

Of the millions of goals constantly set in organizations throughout the world, an overwhelming percentage fizzle before they even see the light of day. As we all know, even in our personal lives, merely setting a goal in no way ensures that we will accomplish it—or even that we will stick with it for more than a few days or a week or a month.

The key is to not only set the right goals, but to set up the right execution. Every great team needs a process in order to achieve its top strategic priorities. Without a common language, framework, and system, success in any organization is left to luck, hope, and chance.

Together with our friends at FranklinCovey, we have spent years examining why some teams and organizations execute well and why some don't.

After extensive research and thousands of interviews, assessments, and case studies, the FranklinCovey team has

FIGURE 3.6

3 Leadership Conversations
Transparent Agenda

1 — DESIRED RESULTS

How to Use: Discuss and come to an agreement on each factor listed below.

What needs to be done?

1. What are the team's top two or three goals?

2. How will we measure success?

3. What are your top two or three individual goals — the goals you need to achieve in order to make your contribution?

4. How do your individual goals connect to the team's top goals? Why are your goals important?

5. Are your goals realistic and achievable?

6. How have you translated these goals into plans (i.e., who will do what by when)?

7. How will you measure your success?

Watchouts

- Avoid taking on too many goals.

- Don't be one-sided or dictatorial. Listen with the intent to understand.

boiled the conclusions down to a simple yet robust approach to help any willing leader learn to execute.

> If you execute, you can do anything. When a company has a clear mission, and people know how their individual mission fits into the big picture, everyone paddles in the same direction.
>
> —STEPHEN COOPER

1. **Focus on the Wildly Important.** Narrow your focus to the important goals and measures of success for the organization and team.
2. **Act on the Lead Measures.** Each week identify the most critical and leveraged activities or behaviors that will drive goal achievement.
3. **Keep a Compelling Scoreboard.** Track progress so that team members always know if they are "winning." The numbers should show if you're on track or if you need to do some course correction.
4. **Create a Cadence of Accountability.** Hold individuals and teams accountable with a simple frequent-review process that is candid, positive, and self-directed.*

To see how this approach works, suppose from a Voice Conversation that your Contribution Statement reads as follows:

I want to operate the finest franchise restaurant in the whole chain. All my energy is around growing a great business and giving my very best to my customers.

That would be your overall desired result.

*If you'd like to know more about FranklinCovey's research in this area, see the bestselling book *The 4 Disciplines of Execution* by Chris McChesney, Sean Covey, and Jim Huling.

This statement is fine as far as it goes. But how are you going to get that result? What specific goals do you need to achieve to make it happen?

As you consider the possibilities, you might narrow your focus to the following three high-leverage goals:

- *Increase our base of loyal customers.*
- *Create a team of engaged employees.*
- *Maximize operational effectiveness.*

These are excellent specific and measurable goals. So now you need to figure out how you're going to measure your success. How will you measure customer loyalty? How will you measure employee engagement and operational effectiveness? You will naturally choose your own measures, but whatever they are, they need to be expressed in numbers everyone can understand and can see all the time. You'll also want to make sure you have your baseline measures in place. What is your current base of loyal customers? How loyal are your employees now?

Measurable goals might be something like this...

By this time next year, we will:

- *Increase our base of loyal customers from 20 percent to 50 percent.*
- *Increase our employee-engagement numbers from 16 percent to 60 percent.*
- *Reduce food waste from 12 percent to 5 percent.*

With measurement specifics in place, now you're equipped to track each goal over time. Everyone should be able to see progress; and if it's not happening, figure out where you need to change course.

Even with this degree of specificity, however, it's not enough to simply set a couple of goals. You need to regularly identify the most "critical and leveraged" actions you can take to ensure that the goals are achieved. You need to ask questions such as:

- *What actions can we take as a team that are most likely to increase customer loyalty?*
- *What can we do that will have a big impact on employee engagement?*
- *How can we improve our ordering processes to ensure we are throwing away less food?*

Performance Conversations, both with individuals and the team, are great opportunities to come up with ideas for actions that will move you toward your goals. You can experiment with the ideas you come up with and track your success in boosting your numbers.

Weekly Performance Conversations with the team keep everyone focused and on track and accountability clear. People can see how things are going, what needs to change, and how what they're doing is helping the team achieve its goals.

As the guide for "Desired Results" (Figure 3.6) points out, you'll want to ensure you don't take on too many goals. You'll also want to make sure you're listening with real intent to understand team members—not with the intent to push your own agenda.

Let's take a look now at a few of the questions people sometimes have about setting goals and achieving desired results.

WHY ONLY TWO OR THREE GOALS AT THE MOST?

Both experience and research clearly show that narrowing the focus is essential to high performance. The more goals you try to accomplish over, say, a one-year period of time, the less likely you are to accomplish them.

Think about it. If your team has only one to three goals, your chances of hitting them with excellence are pretty high. But if you try to hit four, five, or 10 goals, your success rate will probably go down proportionally.

Now consider setting 11, 12, or 20 goals. You might make some progress, but the law of diminishing returns is eventually going to kick in and you'll accomplish nothing with excellence. (See Figure 3.7.)

Progress in achieving goals is a big motivator in unleashing talent. According to research conducted by Harvard professor Teresa Amabile and researcher Steven J. Kramer:

> Of all the things that can boost emotions, motivation, and perceptions during a workday, the single most important is making progress in meaningful work. And the more frequently people experience that sense of progress, the more likely they are to be creatively productive in the long run. Whether they are trying to solve a major scientific mystery or simply produce a high-quality product or service, everyday progress—even a small win—can make all the difference in how they feel and perform.[10]

So during the Performance Conversation, take the time to be selective. What's truly important? What really has to happen?

FIGURE 3.7

Number of Goals	1–3	4–10	11–20
Goals Achieved With Excellence	1–3	1–2	0

The first principle of exceptional execution is narrowing the focus. A person and a team must be able to clearly differentiate between the "good" and the "great" goals. Good goals have significance, consequence, and value; great goals make all the difference.

Let's go back to the example of the "desired results" in your restaurant business:

> *I want to operate the finest franchise restaurant in the whole chain. All my energy is around growing a great business and giving my very best to my customers.*

People think focus means saying yes to the thing you've got to focus on. But that's not what it means at all. It means saying no to the hundred other good ideas that there are.

—STEVE JOBS

You could come up with a lot of goals for your restaurant: put chrysanthemums in a flower box, polish the tables every day, find the freshest-produce vendor in town. These are all good goals.

But the key question to ask is: What things absolutely *must* be accomplished this year or else nothing else really matters? These things become your *Wildly Important Goals*—or "*WIGs.*" In your restaurant, the goals you've chosen to increase your customer base and create a team of engaged employees are WIGs. If you don't have loyal customers and engaged employees, in the long run, what else is going to matter?

When team members don't have clear WIGs, they usually come up with their own agendas, which are often uncoordinated and way out of alignment with your organizational priorities. Even with the best of intentions, most teams will end up misaligned or riding off in all directions.

AUTHOR NOTE I met once with a group of senior government leaders, the executive team for a newly formed agency with a new mandate. They had already met for days creating their strategic plan, so I did a little experiment: I asked each one separately to share with me the agency's top priorities and key goals. I was fascinated by the responses—they were all over the map! Every single person I asked had a completely different idea of what was wildly important, even though after days of planning, they had assumed they were all on the same page.

All too often, bosses feel like they know what the goals are and so do the employees. Bosses live with the impression that their goals have been clearly communicated. Yet, this is rarely true.

FranklinCovey has researched more than 500,000 individuals and more than 5,000 teams on the topic of goal clarity. This research has included organizations across a wide spectrum of industries, including for-profit, nonprofit, government and military organizations, and educational institutions around the world. On average, only 19 percent of individuals in any organization or team can tell you the organization's top priorities.

Gaining clarity on top goals is a core component of a high-performance organization—and of the Performance Conversation. Your goals are not your job description; everything you do in your job is not a WIG.

You will know when you have effectively provided goal clarity when:

- ▶ You've identified a few critical WIGs—goals that, if not achieved, will make the rest of your efforts irrelevant.
- ▶ These WIGs are specific and measurable.
- ▶ You are confident that the individual's WIGs are in line with the goals and purposes of the organization.

- ▶ The leader and individual performer both agree on the WIGs and are willing to evaluate performance based on specific targets, milestones, and benchmarks along the way.
- ▶ The individual performer feels totally supported, with all the resources needed to achieve his or her WIGs.

You might think these steps are obvious and not worth mentioning, but experience has taught us otherwise. Goal clarity is vital. We must never assume everybody knows and understands the goal.

WHAT ABOUT GOALS THAT COME FROM THE TOP?

Typically, strategic goals do come from the top down—which is fine, as long as team members have the opportunity to own those goals. How can you encourage their engagement?

One powerful way is to involve them in both Voice and Performance Conversations about the goals. Look at the firm's strategic goals and ask, "Why do you think each of these goals is important? What's our role in making these goals happen? How can each of us contribute in our own unique way to accomplishing these goals?"

The more people become aware of these goals and their importance, then focus on what they can do—both collectively and individually—to make them happen, the more positively engaged they become.

> **AUTHOR NOTE** Several years ago I had the opportunity to work with a wonderful supervisor named Penny. We had a performance contract agreement on paper, which helped us build a high-trust relationship. The agreement clearly defined the "desired results" in terms of a clear contribution, WIGs, and success measures.

> Penny believed in me and gave me a platform to achieve the desired results. Because of our Voice Conversation, she was always on the lookout for great client projects, client opportunities, international experiences, and ways to leverage my talents and passions.
>
> She also understood that her role was to identify how I could contribute to the great purposes of the organization. From her I learned how to align my voice to my performance. The result was some of the most productive and personally satisfying work I've ever done.

CAN YOU GET TOO FOCUSED ON A GOAL?

It's entirely possible to get too focused on a goal—and then you end up with a "focus paradox" on your hands. You're putting your best energies into a goal you know is most important, but at the same time you develop tunnel vision, and this can create huge problems.

One practical way for leaders to balance focus and awareness is to regularly draw back and ask, "What's going on around us? Are there opportunities or challenges I need to discover more about or pay more attention to?" One benefit of the Leadership Conversations—particularly Performance Conversations—is that they free you up to do that kind of scanning. Once everyone is clear on the most important priorities and fully engaged in them, you're liberated from the feeling that you have to micromanage people.

Step 2: Guidelines

Have you ever found yourself in a situation when you had a "head of steam" to get something done, but kept running into unpleasant surprises that held you back?

There are plenty of pitfalls out there that can prevent you from moving forward with your goals. That's one reason a strong leader always includes in the Performance Conversation a good discussion about guidelines. (See Figure 3.8.)

FIGURE 3.8

3 Leadership Conversations
Transparent Agenda

2−GUIDELINES

How to Use: Discuss and come to an agreement on each factor listed below.

What standards need to be met?

1. What other people need to be involved in this conversation, and what are their expectations?

2. How will your work impact other teams or functions?

3. What policies and/or procedures are in place?

4. Are there any related ecological, quality, safety, or legal requirements to consider?

5. Are there any political or cultural dynamics to consider?

Watchouts

- Don't create unnecessary policies.
- Don't ignore essential policies.

As you engage in Performance Conversations with your team or with individual members of the team, consider addressing issues such as these:

- *What other people need to be involved in this conversation, and what are their expectations?*
- *How will your work impact other teams or functions?*
- *What policies and/or procedures are in place?*
- *Are there any related ecological, quality, safety, or legal requirements to consider?*
- *Are there any political or cultural dynamics to consider?*

One way to get at issues is to play "What if...?" Here are a few examples:

- What if there are some legal issues we are not aware of? How will we deal with them when they arise?
- What if one of us is in a situation where we need to make a "command decision" that may alter our agreement? How will we deal with it?
- What if there are some political issues we are not aware of? How will we deal with them?

The answers to these questions may be quick and easy. Or you may not know the answers, in which case you both need to find out.

Let's go back to your "desired results" in the restaurant business to get a sense of the importance of dealing with guidelines in Performance Conversations.

You focused in on the following high-leverage goals:

- *Increase our base of loyal customers.*
- *Create a team of engaged employees.*
- *Maximize operational effectiveness.*

If some kind of effort to accomplish similar goals in the past has failed—perhaps under prior management—it could be very helpful for you to find out why and include it in your discussion. Your conversation may well lead to ways to save a lot of effort, and in the process, gain some champions.

If there are potential legal or environmental issues, Performance Conversations that result in a good understanding of these issues up front may save some costly errors. Or with the insights of advisors and specialists, you may come up with an entirely new or improved approach that exceeds expectations.

Are there organizational policies that might get in the way? Maybe your company won't let you refund money or give big discounts to help you recover from customer issues. Maybe your budget won't let you hire enough people to do what really should be done for the customer. Performance Conversations to get these issues out on the table could make a big difference in achieving your desired results. What are the nonnegotiable guidelines? Where do you have some flexibility? Is it possible to get the guidelines changed? If so, how?

Always keep in mind that there is a big difference between a principle and a policy. A principle is a natural law. It is timeless, universal, and unchangeable. A policy is a decision made by people about the way things are to be done in certain circumstances, and can be set aside or changed when it isn't working.

When Jean-François Zobrist took over a struggling auto-parts manufacturer called FAVI, he found that the company was hampered by dozens of policies that slowed down the work. For example, workers were not allowed to use a tool without filling out a form and checking the tool out of a locked closet. Why? Because once upon a time, a drill disappeared from the closet. Since management didn't trust the workers, nonsensical policies were keeping them from doing their jobs. Zobrist did away with such policies. He opened the closet and told the workers he trusted them to put things back—and they did.[11]

As a leader, you may need to consider changing policies that aren't based on principles and just get in the way. Or you may need to question organizational policies that unnecessarily complicate or delay the accomplishment of desired results.

As the "watchouts" on the guide for this part of the conversation suggest, you don't want to create policies that are unnecessary. You also don't want to ignore policies that are truly essential.

One construction company we worked with was having a serious problem with accidents on the worksite. Not only were workers getting injured, but the company faced losing its accident insurance. In Performance Conversations, discussions were held around which safety policies needed to be constantly enforced. Everyone agreed on the use of things such as hard hats and steel-toed boots. They also agreed to enforce these policies with each other—to be diligent and aware of them. The result was a big drop in safety incidents.

So you want to appropriately focus on policies that are essential; just make sure everyone clearly understands them. Generally, when people understand the need for a policy, they'll willingly comply with it. You can use Performance Conversations to involve people in recognizing or creating essential policies and then cooperatively enforcing them.

The importance of having good conversations about guidelines is often unrecognized. But these conversations are important in helping people understand the parameters within which they need to operate and look for ways to turn potential stumbling blocks into stepping-stones.

In most cases, this part of the Performance Conversation does not take long, but it does require very open and candid communication. By being proactive in this part of the conversation, leaders can not only avoid pitfalls, but they also can gain helpful information and support for what they are working to accomplish.

Step 3: Resources

Another factor that can throw performance off track is the lack (or perceived lack) of resources. Typically, people never feel like they have enough resources. And often they don't. Nevertheless, the job needs to be done.

It's critical to talk about resources in a Performance Conversation in order to plan wisely, brainstorm possibilities, and make sure there's no misunderstanding down the road. The reason many business goals fail is because people don't sit down first and count the cost of successful execution. (See Figure 3.9.)

In the "resources" part of the Performance Conversation, you can clear up issues such as:

- ▶ Timelines and deadlines
- ▶ Expense budget
- ▶ Capital outlay, if any
- ▶ Information—sources and availability
- ▶ Knowledge—who has it?
- ▶ Training opportunities
- ▶ Facilities/equipment
- ▶ In-house head count (employees)
- ▶ Outsourced work (other labor)
- ▶ Key stakeholder support

FIGURE 3.9

3 Leadership Conversations
Transparent Agenda

3—RESOURCES

How to Use: Discuss and come to an agreement on each factor listed below.

Who/what is needed to accomplish the desired results?

1. What people and other resources (e.g., information, financial, training, etc.) are needed and available?

2. Who can authorize access to the necessary resources?

3. What potential barriers need to be resolved?

4. Is there "game-changing" information or technology that could be utilized?

5. Are there any people or resources that could be repurposed?

Watchouts

- Don't give up too quickly. Is there a different way to obtain the necessary resources?

Together with the members of your team, you can consider questions such as these:

1. What people and other resources (e.g., information, financial, training, and so forth) are needed and available?
2. Who can authorize access to the necessary resources?
3. What potential barriers need to be resolved?
4. Is there "game-changing" information or technology that could be utilized?
5. Are there people or resources that could be repurposed?

Many leaders work to help team members set goals, but when the topic of scarce resources comes up, everything falls apart: "Well, that's just the way things are." "Life is tough." "Figure out your own resources." "You need to make it happen anyway." The implication is that if you're not a "can-do" person, the boss will find someone who is.

In a cavalier way, managers often say something like, "Our people are better than they think. They have more talent and capacity than they know, and it will come out when the pressure is on."

It's an interesting paradox. The manager is right about this. But to abandon team members without a clear idea of what resources they can count on creates stress, confusion, and limitations that significantly complicate execution and actually block the release of talent and capacity.

Is it true that, when pressed, people are capable of more than their current level of performance? Absolutely. However, when they feel they are *forced* into a survival situation, they may do what it takes, but they'll resent every minute of it. They may withdraw the extra capacity as soon as possible, and start planning on leaving—or worse, "getting even" in one way or another.

> What every employer is looking for is not someone who can do the job, but someone who can reinvent the job.
>
> —THOMAS FRIEDMAN

You will actually build a more trusting relationship with the team if you have open, transparent, and frank conversations about available resources.

Let's look at one of your sample goals in the restaurant business: "Improve customer loyalty."

Could you repurpose some funds and budget some training for your team? Could you explore some of the newer, more efficient technologies for measuring customer loyalty? Are there team members who could be assigned as part of their job to follow up with customers and find out what you could do better?

As the watchouts on the Resources Guide suggest, don't give up too quickly. Keep brainstorming. Maybe there's a different way to get what you need. With a little ingenuity, you may come up with resources that don't appear on the surface. Get into the Performance Conversation: "What are our *hidden* resources—people, tools, equipment, sponsors?"

Based on the conversation, you might need to revisit the "desired results" statement and adjust it in light of the resources that are realistically available. You might need to "reinvent" the job to be done to fit your resources.

Conversely, you might "reinvent" the resources. For example, what more do your people really know? Who do they really know? Who may be within their social networks, which are almost always larger than they think? There might be someone somewhere who can help—some resource no one has even thought about yet.

Step 4: Accountability

Holding people accountable is not something you "do" to them. It isn't punitive micromanagement where you play "gotcha" games. It's how leaders help people know how they're doing. And it can be done in a way that is both encouraging and engaging.

Accountability is related to the word "count." It involves looking at the numbers so people can see if they're winning or losing. But it's about more than that. It's a time when people can share and celebrate success, receive recognition for positive effort, and get counsel and help when course correction is needed. It's an important part of a Performance Conversation that happens *between* people. (See Figure 3.10.)

During the "accountability" part of a Performance Conversation, you might ask questions such as the following:

WHAT ARE THE MEASURABLE, INFLUENCEABLE, AND PREDICTIVE ACTIVITIES?

In other words, what activities can you effectively measure and change to move your goals *forward* (rather than simply looking backward to track historical data)?

The numbers that track these activities are called "lead indicators." In working to increase the number of loyal customers in your restaurant, for example, you may decide that the number of times you offer discounts or the average time between when an order is received and when it's filled could significantly influence the number of loyal customers you have, so you make these figures your lead indicators.

If the numbers start to get worse, you can use the "accountability" part of your Performance Conversation to focus on finding out why. If you're working to improve currently fair

FIGURE 3.10

3 Leadership Conversations
Transparent Agenda

4 — ACCOUNTABILITY

How to Use: Discuss and come to an agreement on each factor listed below.

How will we track performance?

1. What are the measurable, influenceable, and predictive activities (lead indicators)?

2. Who will receive information and how will tracking take place?

3. What key milestones will be achieved along the way?

4. How often will we meet to review progress?

5. If necessary, how will we modify our agreement?

Watchouts

- Don't forget that accountability is a two-way, agreement-based process. It is something you *share*, not something you *do* to someone.

- Don't assume that frequent accountability will take place without a systematized communication and review process.

- Don't use accountability as a threat. Instead, use it as a process for creating meaning and engagement.

numbers, you can use it to focus on new ways to do so. You could ask questions such as:

- ▶ "What more enticing discounts could we offer?"
- ▶ "How could we more effectively advertise our discounts?"
- ▶ "How can we best measure order-delivery time on a daily basis?"
- ▶ "What actions are within our power to shorten delivery time?"

WHO WILL RECEIVE INFORMATION AND HOW WILL TRACKING TAKE PLACE?

Goals are often best achieved when people report results to the team as well as their bosses. In working to accomplish your WIGs in your restaurant business, you might want to set up a scoreboard to track the most important numbers, such as lead indicators and WIG measures.

Based on the job to be done, you might also want to talk about key milestones, points where evaluation would be helpful, specific times to review progress, and ways to modify your agreement if necessary.

Unless you have conversations that address issues such as these, people don't know how to measure or account for their efforts.

In some ways, accountability is like keeping score in an athletic game. People tend to disengage for three reasons: (1) they don't know what game they're playing, (2) they don't know whether they're winning or losing, or (3) they can't tell what to do to positively impact the score.

But these things are essential to high performance. In one way or another, "winning" is important to almost everyone. A recent Harvard study on performance and engagement asked the question, "What is the number-one motivating factor for people at work?" The answer? People want to feel a sense of accomplishment in their work. They want to "win."

As former CEO of GE, Jack Welch, has taught:

"Winning in business is great because when companies win, people thrive and grow. There are more jobs and more opportunities everywhere and for everyone. People feel upbeat about the future; they have the resources to send their kids to college, get better healthcare, buy vacation homes, and secure a comfortable retirement. And winning affords them the opportunity to give back to society in hugely important ways beyond just paying more taxes—they can donate time and money to charities and mentor in inner-city schools, to name just two. Winning lifts everyone it touches—it just makes the world a better place."[12]

Figuratively speaking, the "accountability" part of a Performance Conversation empowers people to "win"—to understand the game, to know when they're winning or losing, and to work together to figure out ways to increase the score.

Fundamentally, accountability is about making and reporting on commitments around leading indicators. To do that, we need to:

1. Look at the numbers.
2. Decide whether the leading indicators are actually working.
3. Make new commitments around new or better leading indicators.

Another way to look at the value of conversations about accountability is in terms of paths, landmarks, and destinations.

> **AUTHOR NOTE** My family loves to hike a local trail on a nearby mountain. The trail ends at a well-known landmark, which is easily seen from the valley floor but impossible to see while actually on the hike. In fact, the landmark is not visible until the last few feet of the trail. I really suffer on this hike. It seems to last forever. Every step of the trail looks the exact same as the last. I don't like not knowing where I am on the path and how much farther I have to go until I reach my destination. It would be a lot nicer if I had a few milestones to go by, and if I could see the end getting closer!

The "accountability" part of Performance Conversations helps people know what the end of the journey looks like, keeps them on track, and enables them to understand the significance of each milestone along the way.

To be effective, these conversations need to be held frequently and regularly. They can be brief—20 minutes or less—but they need to be held on a set schedule. Otherwise, people will get off track, and it's surprising how quickly that can happen. Even five-minute stand-up meetings like daily huddles or hallway conversations can do the job.

> **AUTHOR NOTE** I knew a father once who asked his teenage daughter to clean her room on a certain day each week, and he promised he would inspect her room on that day. It worked for a while, but then one week the father had to leave town on inspection day, and he didn't even think about the inspection. The next week when he went to inspect the room, he found it in shambles. When he asked his daughter why the room was such a mess, she asked, "Oh, are we still doing that?" Because he had neglected to keep his part of the bargain, she had forgotten to keep hers.

A best practice is to faithfully hold conversations about accountability either one-on-one or with the whole team at least weekly. A brief conversation might follow this agenda:

▶ **Do some celebrating.** Point out small wins along the way to keep people engaged and also help you to decide which actions are actually making a difference. Call those positive actions out and reinforce them. Because many people have negative feelings when they hear the word "accountability," do lots of complimenting, asking positive questions, brainstorming for ideas, and respecting those ideas.

▶ **Review commitments.** What did people commit to do last week? How did they do? Did their actions improve performance?

▶ **Make new commitments.** Do this in a two-step fashion. Let people propose their own commitments first before you make any suggestions.

As you hold conversations about accountability, keep in mind that they are not only essential to getting to desired results, they're also a great way to keep people engaged in their jobs and feeling like they're making a difference. It's not that people *have* to account; it's that they *get* to account. And that should be a positive experience for leaders and team members alike.

These conversations are also a great way to build trust. In the language of Stephen R. Covey, they give us a chance to make "deposits" in the Trust Accounts we have with leaders and co-workers. They are about making and keeping commitments, celebrating small wins along the way and, when needed, having the honest, candid, and respectful conversations when things are off track. All of these things build trust.

As the watchouts on the Accountability Guide suggest:

▶ Don't forget that accountability is a two-way, agreement-based process. It is something you *share*, not something you *do* to someone.

▶ Don't assume that frequent accountability will take place without a systematized communication-and-review process.

▶ Don't use accountability as a threat. Instead, it is a process for creating meaning and engagement.

Step 5: Consequences

In Performance Conversations, the discussion about consequences should almost always be about "wins." What's a win for the organization? What's a win for the individual? What's a win for you, the leader? And oh, by the way, what happens if we *lose*? When discussing consequences, you might ask:

1. When goals are achieved, what are the implications:
   * *For the customer (internal/external)?*
   * *For the organization?*
   * *For the team?*
   * *For the individual?*
   * *For other stakeholders?*

2. If goals are not achieved, what are the implications:
   * *For the customer (internal/external)?*
   * *For the organization?*
   * *For the team?*
   * *For the individual?*
   * *For other stakeholders?*

3. To get the positive consequences of achieving our goals, do we need to modify the agreement? (See Figure 3.11.)

In your restaurant, for example, what will happen if you accomplish your goals? What will be the result if you do increase your loyal base of customers, create an engaged workforce, and maximize operational effectiveness?

FIGURE 3.11

3 Leadership Conversations
Transparent Agenda

5 — CONSEQUENCES

How to Use: Discuss and come to an agreement on each factor listed below.

1. When goals are achieved, what are the implications:
   - For the customer (internal/external)?
   - For the organization?
   - For the team?
   - For the individual?
   - For other stakeholders?

2. If goals are not achieved, what are the implications:
   - For the customer (internal/external)?
   - For the organization?
   - For the team?
   - For the individual?
   - For other stakeholders?

3. Are modifications to the agreement needed?

Watchouts

- Avoid creating unintended expectations.

> The Emotional Bank Account is a metaphor for the amount of trust that exists in relationships—both personal and professional. Deposits build and repair trust. Withdrawals break down and lessen trust.
>
> Everyone is an accountant. We track the deposits and withdrawals that others make with us, and they do the same with us.
>
> —STEPHEN R. COVEY

Likely, you'll have increased profits, more happy customers, and more word-of-mouth advertising from these happy customers. You'll have more employees who enjoy their work, do a better job at it, and look for ways to make the restaurant even more successful. You may have more money to invest in employee raises, more camaraderie in the workforce, less absenteeism, and fewer employee complaints. Your employees will almost surely have greater trust in you as a leader—trust that you genuinely care about them and have their best interests as well as the interests of the business at heart.

These are significant positive consequences, and articulating them can go a long way toward increasing everyone's incentive to accomplish them.

Now, what will happen if you fail to reach your goals—if you don't increase your customer base or invest in creating an engaged workforce?

You may continue with the status quo—with your current level of business, current profits, current level of employee disengagement, absenteeism, complaints, and lack of trust. Or your customer base may dwindle—or you may even go out of business if some other restaurant in the area offers better food, better deals, and happier, more engaged employees to serve their customers. Besides that, you'll miss out on all the positive consequences you identified.

When you talk about consequences with the people on your team, be sure to talk about the kind of rewards and recognition that are meaningful to the individual contributors and to the team as a whole. It's not just a matter of "carrot and stick." Money is important—but recognition, voice opportunity, and camaraderie often count for more than money. Discuss together some exciting ways you can recognize people when they keep their commitments and execute with excellence. This is where compensation can be tied to performance.

As a watchout, you'll want to avoid creating unintended expectations. You don't want team members planning on a week in Tahiti when all you were thinking of was a team party at the lake on Saturday to celebrate the accomplishment of a goal.

Also, remember that people are unique and need to be rewarded in unique ways. Tickets to a sports event might mean a lot to some and nothing to others. Tailor the consequences to the person (or people) involved.

Formal Performance Conversations With Individuals

Now that we've looked at each of the five elements of the Performance Conversation in depth, let's draw back and look at the conversation as a whole.

Fundamentally, a Performance Conversation is simple and straightforward: choose what needs to be done and how it is to be tracked, then make commitments and report on those commitments. That's about it. But it is a critical tool in the toolkit of a professional leader.

So how do you start?

As with each of the Leadership Conversations, the Conversation Guides provide a simple tool leaders can use to make it happen. Not only do they contain key questions for the conversation, they also provide an open agenda that creates a sense of doable purpose and trust.

You might start with something like this:

"Jackie, do you have an hour today when the two of us could talk together about what we're focused on and how we can help each other? Let's block out that time and see how it goes."

When you meet with her, hand her a set of the guide cards and say, "This is a set of Conversation Guides I've been given to help us ask some relevant questions and focus our time. You'll notice that these cards are called 'transparent agendas,' so you'll be looking at the same cards I'm looking at. Let's take a look at these cards together and see how the questions on each of them might help us.

"Let's start by looking at the statement on this first card. It says the intent of this conversation is 'to improve performance by creating an agreement that establishes priority, focuses effort, clarifies process, and develops trust.' How do you feel about those outcomes? Do you think those things would be helpful for us to do?"

After Jackie responds, you could say, "Now let's look at the five things we need to agree on in order to make that happen." You might point to each of the elements on the guide as you speak.

- ▶ "Desired results" will describe what we want to work together to accomplish.
- ▶ "Guidelines" are the parameters we need to work within—things like policies, procedures, legal, or safety requirements and so on.

▶ "Resources" are the things we have to work with—things like budget, tools, and people.

▶ "Accountability" is about how and when we keep track of our progress. I especially like this part of the conversation because we'll get to celebrate together all the progress we're making and good things that are happening.

▶ "Consequences" will help us identify the positive results we'll get if we accomplish our goals, as well as the negative results if we don't.

"Do you think it would be helpful for us to have clear agreement on each of these things?"

Assuming Jackie is on board, you could say, "Okay. Let's get started. If it would be helpful, here's a tool you can use to take notes as we talk. It may take a few meetings for us to get all this worked out, but eventually I'd like for both of us to have a copy of your performance agreement so we can literally 'be on the same page' as we move forward."

Then you simply start down the list. Talk about each of the five elements in turn. Listen to Jackie's ideas and give input all along the way. Remember, this is a *conversation*—not a monologue—and the goal is an agreement that represents a "win" for Jackie as well as the organization. When you're open about the purpose of the conversation and you both have a set of the guides, you'll find it creates an environment of trust that invites sharing and mutual effort to get the desired results that will benefit everyone. (See Figure 3.12.)

Again, what needs to happen is twofold: to create the performance agreement and to set the tone for ongoing Performance Conversations. This tone can be developed in the way you handle the formal Performance Conversation itself. It can also be developed through brief conversations and

FIGURE 3.12 (See completed sample in Figure 3.13, p. 110.)

WIN-WIN PERFORMANCE AGREEMENT

Agreement Between _____   **Date** _____

Contribution Statement:

Desired Results
What are the results you are trying to achieve?
_____
_____
_____
_____

Guidelines
What key criteria, standards, policies, or procedures should be followed?
_____
_____
_____
_____

Resources
What people, budget, and tools are available?
_____
_____
_____
_____

Accountability
How will we give feedback? How often?
_____
_____
_____
_____

Consequences
What are the rewards if the agreement is fulfilled?
_____
_____
_____
_____

What are the consequences if the agreement is not fulfilled?
_____
_____
_____
_____

helpful interactions in between the formal sit-down Performance Conversations.

As you create the environment in which Leadership Conversations are the norm, ideally Jackie and others would sometimes initiate Performance Conversations.

Formal Performance Conversations With Teams

A formal Performance Conversation with a team follows the same format as one with an individual, but it expands the opportunity to get input from and create buy-in, synergy, and engagement with everyone working on a project or goal. Let's follow a team conversation to see how it might play out.

In this scenario, Kim, who runs a division of a medium-size company, is dealing with a new challenge/opportunity; but he's also dealing with some issues within the team.

Kim's customers have been asking him a long time for a way to do business online. He's been trying to meet with the team and get things going but has run into difficulties. It's become obvious there is neither unity nor clarity around the project.

Things get worse when the team starts talking "accountability"—that is, pointing fingers and blaming each other for the breakdowns in the project.

What would happen if Kim were to hold a Performance Conversation with the team, and how would he do it?

He could call his team together and give each person a set of the Performance Conversation Guides. He could go through the same process we talked about going through with Jackie in the previous example in explaining and addressing the important performance questions.

As he tries to work with the people on the team who already have issues with blaming and accusing, he may encounter divergent opinions, even on the value of going through the process. But in the spirit of the Performance Conversation, he could listen carefully for understanding. He could demonstrate trust in the people on the team and communicate respect for their views and a real desire to hear them out.

He might say something like this: "I can see that there are differences of opinion here and some of you question the value of going through this process. Let me ask you a question. If we were able to get all of these issues out on the table, to address these differences head-on and come to the point where we could Synergize together and come to a clear agreement on each of these five areas, do you think it would make a difference in our ability to achieve what we want and need to achieve? Do you think it would improve our performance as a team?"

Assuming there is some degree of positive response, Kim might then say, "Would you be willing to give it a try? This process gives us an open agenda—you'll be looking at the same cards I'm looking at. Why don't we just try going through the questions on these cards and see if we can get a process going that will enable us to create that kind of synergy?"

At that point, Kim may be able to move forward with the formal Performance Conversation. If resentment runs deep and it becomes clear that the "voices" of some team members are not being heard, he may need to move back to individual Voice Conversations in order to prepare team members for this kind of synergy.

Whenever Kim reaches the point of consensus on moving forward with the Performance Conversation, he can facilitate a discussion of the five elements, and with the combined talents and interactive engagement of everyone involved, the team can come up with clarity and agreement in each of these areas that will significantly improve their ability to focus on and accomplish the desired results.

In the process, they can learn how important it is to clarify expectations with each other. They can learn that in order to perform, they must make commitments to each other.

They can discover they have many opportunities to influence the scope of the project. Instead of complaining about the lack of resources, they can work to discover hidden resources.

They can learn that accountability is less about "holding someone's feet to the fire" than it is about keeping commitments to each other.

They can also learn the age-old truth that we truly find *self* only when we move *beyond self*. When people work together toward something meaningful, synergy ignites and great things happen. This is the stuff that kindles fire.

Again, the process may well take more than one Performance Conversation—particularly in working with a group. And follow-up is critical. If leaders don't take the process through to completion, they will lose credibility. But all of these interactions will not only help resolve the immediate issues, they will also help to create the desired environment of ongoing team Performance Conversations. (See Figure 3.13.)

Creating a Culture of Informal Performance Conversations

Certainly, formal Performance Conversations, where you come up with written performance agreements, are essential. But as we've said, it's in the culture of informal Performance Conversations that top performance actually happens. This is where you create a culture of performance rather than a culture of performance reviews. This is where the effective leader can

FIGURE 3.13

WIN-WIN PERFORMANCE AGREEMENT

Agreement Between VP of Sales and Jackie   **Date** September 1

Contribution Statement
I will bring my deep project-management expertise and people-leadership skills to help my department and our company achieve our sales goals.

Desired Results
What are the results you are trying to achieve?
• To be an effective project leader with full ownership for training of account executives on a new "go to market" approach of our product.
• To meet quarterly and meet annual sales goals with new products.
• To engage in new and challenging opportunities that provide ongoing learning and development experiences.

Guidelines
What key criteria, standards, policies, or procedures should be followed?
• Weekly communication with Sales and Marketing leaders are to be attended in person.
• Training on the new product must be done while the current product continues to be successfully marketed and sold.

Resources
What people, budget, and tools are available?
• Administrative assistance from the sales leader's current support staff.
• Predetermined budgets for training and ongoing coaching meetings.
• 10 to 15 hours a week of assistance from existing members of the training team.

Accountability
How will we give feedback? How often?
• Weekly update meetings will be held each Monday where progress will be shared.
• The Product Rollout Scoreboard will be updated daily with current information.
• A monthly meeting with the sales leader will be held to review the overall progress and make any needed adjustments.

Consequences
What are the rewards if the agreement is fulfilled?
• The company hits and exceeds revenue targets for new product.
• I gain additional experience with new opportunities using the previously "untapped" talent.
• I receive bonus pay tied to the success of revenue targets.

What are the consequences if the agreement is not fulfilled?
• Both the company and I fail to receive the positive consequences listed above.

address performance issues immediately. As UCLA's Professor Samuel A. Culbert points out, "It's much better for everyone involved to talk about the important issues when there's still time to take action, to fix what's going wrong."[13] With a formal performance agreement in place, you already have the context for the conversation, as well as a relationship with some degree of trust.

Though an informal Performance Conversation may only last a few minutes, you can still address all five elements effectively. For example, suppose Gavin—a cashier in your restaurant—has been late every day for his shift. Because of your formal Performance Conversation with him, he already knows the desired results and guidelines of his job.

You might pull him aside and say, "Gavin, can we talk? If we're going to accomplish our desired results, we need you to be on time for your shift. Can you tell me what's going on?" You'll want to show respect, to listen, and to make sure you understand the full story.

Gavin tells you he has a college class that gets out late every day, and sometimes he misses his bus.

You might then say, "What are your resources for changing that?"

Gavin starts thinking. "I guess I could explain to the teacher that I just have to leave on time. Or I could catch a ride to work with Jimmy instead of waiting for the bus." Let him seek out his own hidden resources and make his own commitments to you.

"That sounds good, Gavin. Let's try that, and then let's check back in a couple of days to see how it's going. From there we can decide what to do."

Sometimes a Performance Conversation is as simple as that; but note how, even in an informal conversation such as this, it's possible for a leader to deal with all five elements of the conversation. Note, too, how even with a seemingly mundane issue such as arriving late for a shift, an informal Performance Conversation can begin to unleash a person's ability to problem-solve and be more self-reliant.

Often you can also unleash potential by using an informal Performance Conversation to tie in to the elements of "voice."

"Jan, I noticed you seemed concerned and maybe a little frustrated by the reports we received about some quality issues with our last shipment to [Company X]. I know you invested a lot of yourself in the development of that product and you really believe it meets an important need. Can you tell me a little more about your concern?"

"Well, yeah. I really did work hard on that, and I can't believe that shipment had so many problems."

"I can tell this is really important to you. What resources are you aware of that could help you resolve the issue?"

"Well, I think I need to start by really analyzing the specific problems and where things went wrong."

"That sounds good. Anything else you can think of?"

"Actually, yes. Once I figure out the source, I'd like to put in writing what I see that needs to happen differently. Do you think you could review it and maybe tell me how to best get that information to the people who need it?"

"Do your research and write up your observations and suggestions. Then let's take a look at it and see where we go from there. How long do you think it will take you to do that?"

"I think I could probably have it done by Wednesday. And you know, as I think about it, I'd also like to come up with some meaningful way to make this up to [Company X]."

"Good idea. Why don't you get everything to me by end of day Wednesday, and we can review it together on Thursday morning—say around 9 o'clock? I think your desire to get on this right away could make a big difference in keeping

[Customer X] happy and also in making sure guidelines are in place to prevent this from happening in the future."

As Jan feels reconnected and reinforced in her passion and efforts to contribute, and that her suggestions are valued and heard, she becomes more engaged and more focused on improving performance—her own and that of the company as well.

Again, these informal Performance Conversations are where the rubber meets the road. In one sense, the formal performance agreement is like a game plan, but the game is actually played hour by hour, day by day in light of the plan. As with each of the other Leadership Conversations, success in performance is not in having a *conversation*; it's about creating an *environment* of ongoing conversations around the elements that create high-performance individuals and organizations.

Performance Conversation Watchouts

We've already brought up a few specific watchouts as we've looked at each of the five elements of the performance agreement. In the big picture, you'll also want to watch out for the following as you hold Performance Conversations:

- ▶ Assuming people know where to focus.
- ▶ Listening to reply rather than understand.
- ▶ Failing to differentiate between the *many important tasks* and the *vital few*.
- ▶ Failing to make specific links to overall organizational objectives.
- ▶ Giving superficial attention to issues, questions, and challenges.
- ▶ Pushing your agenda rather than seeking mutual agreement.

You might take a minute now to honestly examine your own beliefs and behaviors. Do any of these watchouts describe the way you think or the things you do? If so, they'll get in the way of your ability to help your team achieve top performance.

As you avoid these watchouts—as you recognize the need to help people know where to focus; genuinely listen to understand; learn to discern and focus on the vital few tasks that really make the difference; help team members create links between their work and the overall objectives of the organization; give serious attention to issues, questions, and challenges; and always seek mutual agreement rather than pushing your own agenda—you'll be amazed at the talent you can unleash and the level of performance you and your team can achieve. (See Figure 3.14.)

Final Thoughts

In an office somewhere, possibly even right now, people are talking about failure.

> ▶ "We were just working on the wrong priorities."
> ▶ "I had no idea what was expected of me."
> ▶ "That time frame was totally unrealistic."
> ▶ "I didn't have the support or resources I needed to be successful."
> ▶ "We had all of the responsibility but no authority to act."
> ▶ "The budget was too small. No wonder the project failed."

If you are building a culture where honest expectations are communicated and peer accountability is the norm, then the group will address poor performance and attitudes.

—HENRY CLOUD

FIGURE 3.14

3 Leadership Conversations
Transparent Agenda

PERFORMANCE CONVERSATION WATCHOUTS

Avoid

- Assuming people know where to focus.
- Listening to reply rather than to understand.
- Failing to differentiate between the *many important tasks* and the *vital few.*
- Failing to make specific links to overall organizational objectives.
- Giving superficial attention to issues, questions, and challenges.
- Pushing your agenda rather than seeking mutual agreement.

Unfortunately, such side conversations are all too common. What a waste of time, effort, and resources when people are not absolutely clear, engaged, and on the same page!

Performance Conversations transform both the nature and the results of the communication that goes on in an organization. As you engage in these conversations, in time you may hear comments such as this: "A lot of what we used to talk about around here was pretty much useless or even negative. Now our conversations have a sense of purpose—not only about the task at hand, but about why it's important to the company and why it's important to each of us. Frankly, it helps me feel I'm part of something important and not just putting in my time."

Whether formal or informal, Performance Conversations build hope and encouragement. They signal that you genuinely care about every member of the team; that you want to engage the fullest contribution from every voice; that the wins of team members matter as much to you as the wins for the organization; and that you want to ensure all the major elements of successful performance are clearly articulated.

As with Voice Conversations, Performance Conversations put work and relationships in context, and that context gives meaning. They unleash the talent of individuals and teams so that all team members have the best possible chance to succeed in accomplishing Wildly Important Goals.

DISCUSSION QUESTIONS

1. How does "voice" relate to a performance agreement with an individual? With a team?
2. How do you think Performance Conversations can be motivating?
3. What could you do if someone says, "Just tell me what to do. I don't want to waste time talking about it"?
4. How might you develop a performance agreement with a worker who hasn't earned a lot of trust yet?
5. What could you do as a leader if you don't agree with the other person on his or her view of some element in the agreement?
6. What can you do if your boss doesn't initiate a Performance Conversation?

7. When and how might you modify elements in an agreement?
8. How do you think performance agreements can develop trust?
9. Why might people be fearful of a Performance Conversation? How can you help dispel those fears?
10. How would you fill in the five elements of a performance agreement with your own supervisor?
11. What do you think is the difference between a job description and an effective performance agreement?
12. When might it not be a good idea to hold a Performance Conversation?

CHAPTER 4

THE CLEAR-THE-PATH CONVERSATION

It is the leader's job to clear the path of obstacles, ensuring that each individual is able to succeed.

—From *The 4 Disciplines of Execution*

In 1957, the Soviet Union shocked the world when it launched the satellite *Sputnik*. The space race was officially on—and the United States was losing!

Two years later, Project Mercury began under the leadership of President Dwight D. Eisenhower. The goal was to orbit a manned spacecraft around the earth in order to investigate and determine the ability of human beings to function in space. Could they launch an astronaut into space? Could they get the astronaut back home safely? Again, the United States lagged behind. On April 12, 1961, Soviet cosmonaut Yuri Gagarin became the first man to orbit the earth. Once again, the United States was in shock—and still losing the space race.

A few days later, President John F. Kennedy stood before the American Congress and spoke these game-changing words:

"Now it is time to take longer strides—time for a great new American enterprise—time for this nation to take a clearly leading role in space achievement, which in many ways may hold the key to our future on earth.

I believe we possess all the resources and talents necessary. But the facts of the matter are that we have never made the national decisions or marshaled the national resources required for such leadership. We have never specified long-range goals on an urgent time schedule, or managed our resources and our time to insure their fulfillment.

I believe that this nation should commit itself to achieving the goal, before this decade is out, of landing a man on the moon and returning him safely to the earth. No single space project in this period will be more impressive to mankind, or more important for the long-range exploration of space; and none will be so difficult or expensive to accomplish. In a very real sense, it will not be one man going to the moon—if we make this judgment affirmatively, it will be an entire nation. For all of us must work to put him there."[1]

Within a year, Alan Shepard and Gus Grissom became the first two Americans to travel into space. On February 20, 1962, John Glenn Jr. became the first American to orbit the earth. In May of 1963, three additional U.S. astronauts orbited the earth. Then it was time to go to the moon. On July 20, 1969, the *Apollo 11* astronauts—Neil Armstrong, Michael Collins, and Edwin "Buzz" Aldrin Jr.—led the mission to land on the moon, fulfilling President Kennedy's vision well within the decade goal he had established.

President Kennedy did not personally build a single rocket. He did not don any space gear. He did not take a single step on the moon. But his vision and his leadership literally "cleared the path" toward the exploration of space. Not only did he create the vision with his stirring words, but he also helped maintain the priority and remove the obstacles by initiating and supporting what needed to happen to bring the vision to reality. Under his leadership, the enormous funding was appropriated, new centers were built, new infrastructure was created, and new systems were put into place. In the ever-changing political environment, he provided the critical ongoing support.

Great leaders are constantly encouraging people, removing obstacles, and spraying the pathway with Teflon, so to speak. And this is true of leaders at every level. Even if you are not the president of anything or in any formal leadership role at all, you can still be in an informal leadership role at work, in your community, and in your home. Leadership is about influence, and the principle of "clearing the path" applies at every level.

Clearing the path is about being a source of help to those around you—especially those you have the chance to lead. It is not about setting up a codependent, bureaucratic, or unempowered relationship or doing for others what they have the power to do and should do for themselves; it's about recognizing a need and opening the way for people to perform at a higher level. (See Figure 4.1.)

There may be something you can do in five minutes that would take an employee five hours to do. You may be in a position to clarify a policy, make an introduction that will create a networking relationship, or even send a simple email that would tear down a significant barrier for someone. Recognize those opportunities. Clear the path for those around you.

Like a compass, the Voice Conversation provides direction for the journey.

Like a scoreboard, the Performance Conversation tells you how you're doing on the journey.

The purpose of the Clear-the-Path Conversation is to remove the obstacles on the path so that talent can be fully

FIGURE 4.1

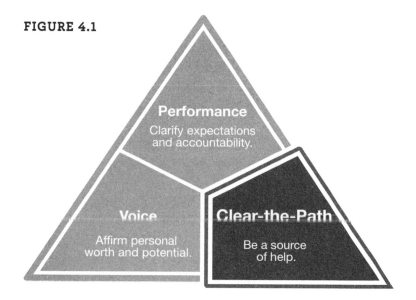

unleashed to reach the destination of the journey with expediency, shared satisfaction, and joy. (See Figure 4.2.)

Pick Your Style, Pick Your Path

Leaders typically adopt one of three roles:

1. **Micromanager**—one who constantly hovers and gives orders, never ceding control or ownership to anyone else. A micromanager actually becomes an obstacle to progress rather than a "path clearer."

2. **Abandoner**—one who hands off responsibilities and then disappears without giving adequate support or resources. Sometimes under the guise of "empowerment," an abandoner will quit the scene, jump ship, ride off into the sunset, and leave team members to struggle alone.

FIGURE 4.2

3 Leadership Conversations
Transparent Agenda

CLEAR-THE-PATH

"Leaders can be a source of help to those they lead.
They can look ahead and try to discern what may be
needed. They can watch and learn from what the team
is doing and see what team members need to keep
going and/or improve. They can then teach or pass
on what they learn. They can coach. They can help
prevent problems and anticipate opportunities. Each
can work within his or her Circle of Influence to help
and support one another. This is how quantum
performance improvement comes."

TALENT UNLEASHED

3. **Clear-the-Path Leader**—one who neither microman-
   ages nor abandons, but runs alongside to support and
   ahead to remove barriers to success.

Let's look at each of these roles a little more closely.

MICROMANAGER

We often say that a micromanager is "detail-oriented." More
accurately, the typical micromanager is an inexperienced or
insecure leader who doesn't trust those he or she leads to do
their jobs right.

In most cases of micromanagement, the manager unilaterally takes over and overrides the performance agreement—if there is one. This action says, "I really didn't trust you to be responsible for this task after all," or "The agreement we made was just talk." It robs team members of the opportunity to succeed in accomplishing goals and responsibilities and of prospects for learning and growth in their work. It throws a wet blanket on creativity and motivation.

Though they don't realize it, micromanagers do themselves no favor as they run themselves ragged shoring up the timbers to keep the structure from falling down. In addition, they fail to develop and position strong successors, creating a leadership vacuum and driving good people away.

As Jim Collins says in his book *How the Mighty Fall*, "Any exceptional enterprise depends first and foremost upon having self-managed and self-motivated people."[2] While we might think great performance requires a lot of rules, policies, and procedures, research suggests just the opposite. Too many rules, policies, and procedures often create rigidity and bureaucracy. The key to unleashing talent is to create a culture of freedom with clear responsibilities and accountability.

> **AUTHOR NOTE** I once had the opportunity to volunteer in a community service project. Overseeing my efforts was an employee who appreciated my time but was also committed to ensuring I made the absolute best use of every minute. Therefore, I was shown the "best way" to wring out a towel and the "best way" to wrap up a vacuum cord. By the time I was finished, I was glad this particular opportunity to serve was a one-time experience. Of course, as my spouse can tell you, my talent for cleaning isn't exactly world-class, but I just wilted under the stern eye of this employee.

Consider the experience of our friend Christine. After working hard for many years, she was promoted to "second in command" of a large division and was excited to begin her new job. She met with the director of the division, who laid out all the key initiatives. Then he proceeded to tell her in great detail exactly how to perform each task, essentially leaving her feeling like a robot without input and personal commitment.

This conversation "zapped out" all of Christine's energetic enthusiasm for the job. She felt as though her creativity and initiative had been squashed. As soon as she was able to transfer, Christine was gone.

Though it may get the immediate job done efficiently, micromanagement stifles any opportunity or motivation for people to develop and unleash their talent. When every action is controlled, monitored, and watched, people respond accordingly. They eventually just sit on their hands and wait to be told what to do. Their voices are stifled. According to Trinity Solutions, "Approximately 69 percent said they considered changing jobs because of micromanagement and another 36 percent actually changed jobs."[3]

Some leaders associate "unleashing" talent with an unacceptable loss of control. "Why would I want people running all over 'unleashed'? Shouldn't people be tightly managed? Shouldn't they be harnessed and under control?" As a result, many organizations are overmanaged and underled. Their leaders simply can't give away even the slightest degree of control.

In his book *Turn the Ship Around!*, David Marquet shares his experience as a U.S. Navy captain just a few days after taking over command of a new nuclear-powered submarine. On their first test run—in the midst of a four-day schedule jammed with training, exercises, and inspections—he decided to take the advice of his engineer and add an engineering drill. This drill would involve shutting down the reactor with a simulated fault, forcing the engineering department to find the problem, do the necessary repairs, and restart the reactor.

The drill was underway and going smoothly when Marquet—a bit nervous due to "inspection mentality" and not wanting his crew to think of their new leader as "easy"—decided to make things a bit more challenging by increasing the speed of the sub. "Ahead two-thirds!" he barked. In his words, "This would significantly increase the rate of battery discharge and put pressure on the troubleshooters to find and correct the fault quickly. At 'ahead two-thirds,' there is a nearly continuous click-click-click on the battery amp-hour meter, an audible reminder that time is running. It's physically unnerving!"

So he gave the order to his executive officer, "Ahead two-thirds!" The officer ordered the helmsman, "Ahead two-thirds!"

And nothing happened. The helmsman didn't move to execute the order; he just squirmed in his seat.

Marquet asked him what was going on.

"Captain," he replied, "there is no 'ahead two-thirds' on the EPM."

This was news to Marquet. He realized that in the midst of all the technical training he'd received in order to command this new submarine, he must have missed it. Every ship he had been on previously had one-third and two-thirds on the motor, so he had simply assumed this one did too.

He pulled his executive officer aside and asked him if he had known the order couldn't be carried out when he gave it.

"Yes, Captain, I did," he said.

Astonished, Marquet said, "Well, why did you order it?"

"Because you told me to," the executive officer replied.

From this experience, Marquet decided to stop giving orders. He knew he had an extremely well-trained crew. He began to let everyone on the ship take care of his own responsibilities, and he helped whenever needed. He taught people to say to him, "Captain, I intend to (do this or that)," and his response was generally, "Very well." If a problem arose, he would expect them to raise the issue with him and get help.[4]

In a crisis, it's tempting to just take control—and sometimes that's necessary. But even in stressed and pressured situations, consider what it means to "unleash" people. They can be more resilient and more responsive than you think.

ABANDONERS

Though more subtle than micromanagement, abandonment also shows disrespect for people and performance agreements. Rather than demonstrating trust, abandoners communicate that they don't care about the people they lead and might even—perhaps unconsciously—be setting them up as scapegoats. This is a particular risk for virtual teams. Because they do not work together physically, it's easy for team members to feel disconnected.

Often a performance review will happen with fanfare, celebration, and lots of good will. But then the manager seems to forget all about it. Day after day, week after week, he or she is nowhere to be found—in a meeting, on a trip, or behind a locked door. The team member hears nothing at all for months—then, all of a sudden, it's time for the next performance review, which the person approaches without any sense of what's actually going to be reviewed.

The "case of the disappearing manager" is a common story in many organizations. Usually, these managers don't intend to disappear—they just feel like they have so much on their plates that they (ironically) can't take time to do their main job: directing and enabling the highest contributions of the people on their team. Sometimes leaders who abandon their people do so under the guise of survival of the fittest. Some managers will say, "When I came to this company, I just had to figure it out for myself. This is how we work out who the winners and the losers are."

It's easy to think of "micromanagers" or "abandoners" as some sinister outside forces infiltrating our organizations. But we could easily find ourselves in both categories—perhaps even at the same time.

For example, suppose we're responsible for a big project. The progress reports we're getting begin to worry us, so we feel we have "no choice" but to grab the controls. It will eat up our time, but we think, "You do what you have to do."

As a result, other projects now get less attention. The people on those projects also need guidance and help along the path, and without it, their projects go off track. Soon we're fighting fires all over the landscape. We become "helicopter managers," swooping in and "saving the day." While this may feed our ego in the short run, in the long run it's punishing for us and everyone else. Helicopter managing is just a manifestation of the pendulum swing from tight control to false empowerment.

So, what's the solution? It's a genuine 3rd Alternative called "Clear-the-Path Leadership."

CLEAR-THE-PATH LEADERS

Clear-the-Path Leaders neither micromanage nor abandon their teams. They don't constantly "snoopervise" and take over when they think things aren't going the way they should. They don't disappear and then suddenly reappear out of nowhere to "fix" what the team has done wrong. Instead, they make themselves *continually available* to help, support, and remove obstacles for team members as they work to accomplish the tasks both they and their leader have agreed they should do. (See Figure 4.3.)

FIGURE 4.3

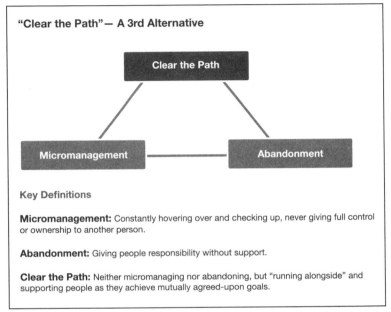

"Clear the Path"— A 3rd Alternative

Clear the Path

Micromanagement ——————— Abandonment

Key Definitions

Micromanagement: Constantly hovering over and checking up, never giving full control or ownership to another person.

Abandonment: Giving people responsibility without support.

Clear the Path: Neither micromanaging nor abandoning, but "running alongside" and supporting people as they achieve mutually agreed-upon goals.

"Clearing the path" does not create codependent relationships where the team is fully dependent on the leader to make all the decisions; neither does it create counterdependent situations where their direct reports have the role and title, but are not fully able to use their role, power, and authority to make decisions. Clearing the path means leaders go way beyond simply removing obstacles and barriers. They offer their people a fully empowered environment and role with the decision-making power, authority, and responsibility to act and influence their work and those they interact with and serve.

The Clear-the-Path Leader shows up for work—not as the boss barking orders, but as an advocate and a facilitator, ready and willing to lend a helping hand.

One way to envision the role of a Clear-the-Path Leader is to picture an icebreaker—a ship whose special purpose is to break up the ice and create a smooth waterway for other ships in the frozen northern seas. An icebreaker has a strong, specially designed hull that splits ice and pushes the debris aside so other vessels can move through. The largest icebreakers are more than 500 feet long and can smash through ice 16 feet thick. With that kind of power, they can keep frozen seaways open year-round for world trade.

To become an ice pilot requires a lot of experience. Pilots need to know how ice behaves, understand the kinds of hazards that might arise, and be able to select the best routes. Ice conditions change all the time—what was easy last year looks hard this year; what looks open now might freeze up in an hour or so and trap the ship. The job of the ice pilot requires intense concentration and alertness.

Another way to envision the role is to imagine a high-functioning American football team. A good running back consistently rushes for more than 1,000 yards per season. He is able to do this because the fullback and key blockers constantly open up holes in the defensive line for him to run through. This is called "rushing offense." The blockers take advantage of split-second opportunities, pushing one way or the other depending on the unpredictable maneuvers of the opposing team. If they do their job well, a good runner should be able to rush more than six yards per play.

Meanwhile, the coach is running alongside, watching closely to learn the other team's patterns of play, figuring out with his experienced eye the best way to get through the opposition. At each opportunity, he's giving input to the team on how to improve.

In business, effective leaders clear the path of barriers to progress so the team can move forward. Their focus is intense.

They're always looking for new and better pathways toward the goal.

Why Hold Clear-the-Path Conversations?

Richard, the president of an oil company in the Northwest, came to realize how much time he was spending doing what others could and should be doing, so he started having regular Performance Conversations with his people, moving more and more responsibility to them.

As he began moving away from day-to-day *management* issues, he found he had time to be a *leader*. He began to spend most of his time clearing the path for others. He looked ahead at the trends in the industry and anticipated obstacles. His conversations with his people turned to helping them navigate their way through major changes hitting the business.

In retrospect, this man's co-workers felt that if the president had not taken the time to clear the path, they would not have been able to respond as effectively as they did in the changing environment and, in fact, the company would likely not even have survived.

Demonstrating the power of Clear-the-Path Leadership in another role, Harvard Business School Professor Clayton M. Christensen shared the following experience in his book *How Will You Measure Your Life?*

> As I look back on my own life, I recognize that some of the greatest gifts I received from my parents stemmed not from what they did for me—but rather, from what they didn't do for me.
>
> One such example: my mother never mended my clothes. I remember going to her when I was in the early grades of elementary school, with holes in both socks of my favorite pair. Our family had no extra money anywhere, so buying

new socks was just out of the question. So she told me to go string thread through a needle, and to come back when I had done it. That accomplished— it took me about 10 minutes, whereas I'm sure she could have done it in 10 seconds— she took one of the socks and showed me how to run the needle in and out around the periphery of the hole, rather than back and forth across the hole, and then simply to draw the hole closed. This took her about 30 seconds. Finally, she showed me how to cut and knot the thread. She then handed me the second sock, and went on her way.

> The quality of the relationship people have with their direct supervisor is a key determinant of the fear—or lack of fear— they experience at work.
>
> —KATHLEEN D. RYAN and DANIEL K. OESTREICH

A year or so later—I probably was in third grade—I fell down on the playground at school and ripped my Levi's. This was serious, because I had the standard family ration of two pairs of school trousers. So I took them to my mom and asked if she could repair them. She showed me how to set up and operate her sewing machine, including switching it to a zigzag stitch, gave me an idea or two about how she might try to repair it if it were she who was going to do the repair, and then went on her way. I sat there clueless at first, but eventually figured it out.

Although in retrospect these were very simple things, they represent a defining point in my life. They helped me to learn that I should solve my own problems whenever possible; they gave me the confidence that I could solve my own problems; and they helped me experience pride in that achievement. It's funny, but every time I put those socks on until they were threadbare, I looked at that repair in the toe and thought, "I did that." I have no memory now of what the repair to the knee of those Levi's looked like, but I'm sure it wasn't pretty. When I looked at it, however, it didn't occur to me that I might not have done a perfect mending job. I only felt pride that I had done it.

How did Professor Christensen's mother clear the path for her son? Simple. When he encountered an obstacle, she showed him in general terms what to do about it and then left him to take care of it himself. Because he overcame the obstacle himself, he took ownership of the solution.

When a leader helps someone but *does not take over*, that person is saying in terms both loud and clear, "This is your responsibility, and I value and trust you. I'm happy to do what I can to help clear the way so that you can do your job." Clearing the path without "taking over" actually strengthens a culture of responsibility and trust. (See Figure 4.4.)

If as a leader you feel overwhelmed with all you have to do and all you need to check up on, distrustful of the people around you, and fearful of failure, it usually means you're not unleashing talent. Instead of clearing the path for others, you're trying to singlehandedly drag them down the path of success.

If you find you have to constantly fix, take over, or just do it yourself, it is time to start holding Voice and Performance Conversations and establishing the conditions that will enable you to spend more time in Clear-the-Path Conversations. In the process, the person you save might just be yourself.

If you have already held effective Voice and Performance Conversations, you don't need to supervise. The agreements do the supervising. Going back to the American football metaphor, when agreements supervise, leaders are free to coach the game instead of playing it themselves. Individual contributors drive themselves toward the goal according to mutually agreed-upon and self-chosen targets, objectives, and measures.

FIGURE 4.4

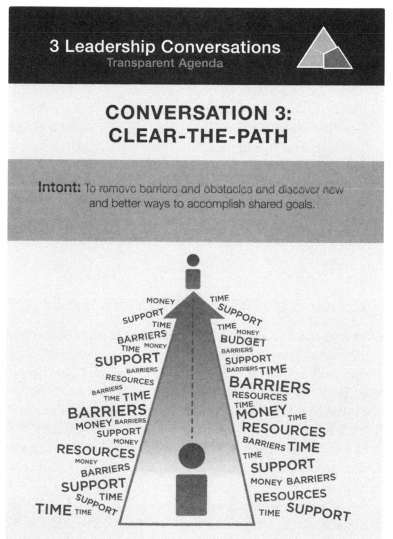

How to Hold Clear-the-Path Conversations

In a Clear-the-Path Conversation, you might want to ask questions such as the following:

1. "What are you working on, and how is it going?"
2. "What are you learning?"
3. "What obstacles are getting in your way?"
4. "If you could change one thing to improve your progress, what would it be?"
5. "What can team members do to remove barriers for each other?"
6. "What new opportunities are you seeing?"
7. "How can I best help you?" (This is one question that should always be asked.) Let's look at each of these questions in greater depth.

WHAT ARE YOU WORKING ON, AND HOW IS IT GOING?

This is *not* an "I'm checking up on you to make sure you're on task" kind of question. The wording of the question assumes team members are making their own decisions about how to use their time. If there's a solid Win-Win Performance Agreement in place, an effective leader will trust them to do so.

When asked with a helpful, even curious tone, the question will not be offensive. It shows that you care and that you invite people to share their issues and concerns—and their victories— with you.

Often they will want to tell you about the good things they're doing. It's wise to take time to listen and celebrate—to help them understand that their wins are just as important to you as they are to them. Through the conversation, team members can teach you how their work is done and show you innovations. They can demonstrate ideas and behaviors you might want to share with others.

On the other hand, they might share concerns. This is good. Your job is to address their concerns and help remove obstacles so they can succeed. Bottlenecks, bureaucracy, lack of resources—you're the one who needs to attend to those things in your leadership role.

> **AUTHOR NOTE** I had two back-to-back jobs once. I'd work in one place in the morning and the other place in the afternoon. My morning boss was always available to help us if we needed her. She would spend some time going from one station to another and we'd just converse about what was going on and how we could move things forward. She didn't interrupt us; she didn't stare over our shoulders. She just took an interest and solved problems we couldn't solve ourselves. In a way, the Clear-the-Path Conversation was ongoing.
>
> My afternoon boss was the opposite. We never saw him unless there was some crisis, and then he was all over us, demanding this and that, and making lots of noise. He considered himself a "hands-on" leader. He was anything but.

As long as you approach Clear-the-Path Conversations with a trusting tone in your voice, you'll find that you can smooth the path and accelerate progress with individuals and with the whole team.

WHAT ARE YOU LEARNING?

It's almost a necessity in today's world for great leaders to be practically obsessed with learning. As everyone knows, the future belongs to the innovators.

In countless articles, books, and TED talks, we hear a lot of complicated philosophy about the "learning organization." It's actually quite simple to define: A learning organization is one in which team members learn something and then share it with others. The leader's job is to make sure learning and sharing happen—and often to be the conduit for that learning.

> **AUTHOR NOTE** In my first job out of college, I noticed my boss had funny posture. When he talked with someone, he always had his head cocked to one side. At first, I thought it was a neck problem, but it wasn't that at all—he was just an intense listener.
>
> The first question this man asked in my hiring interview was, "What do you read?" I was startled because I wasn't expecting a question like that. Fortunately, I do a lot of reading. He liked that, so he hired me on the spot.
>
> Not a day went by that he didn't ask me what was new, exciting, and innovative that he could learn from me. I got into the habit of thinking a lot about my job and how it could be done better, how the business could operate better, and what new opportunities there might be for growing the business.
>
> Through his constant curiosity, our leader made each of us on the team curious too, and the job was a lot more interesting because of it. On top of that, we were always trying new and better ideas—many of which actually changed our business in fundamental ways and for the better.

WHAT OBSTACLES ARE GETTING IN YOUR WAY?

Clearing the path is all about removing obstacles. Like the icebreaker pilot, you're the one who runs interference and keeps the way forward as easy and clear as possible. Your team members live in a kind of fragmented world because their contribution is individual. Anything you can do to align that contribution with the needs of the organization and the marketplace is part of your leadership responsibility. Nothing discourages workers faster than to feel their contribution doesn't matter or isn't making a difference, and if the leader won't help move the barriers out of the way, that's exactly how they will feel.

> One of the most powerful, practical things a leader can ask is, "What's getting in the way?"
>
> —STEVE JACOBS

The most often-cited barriers include:

- *Excessive bureaucracy* (too many confusing processes, too many hoops to jump through, too many people to please)
- *Budget restraints* (never enough money or resources to "do the job right")
- *Battling objectives* (conflicts among people's different priorities)

An effective leader focuses on removing or easing as many of these barriers as possible. Let's look at some ways you might do that.

Excessive Bureaucracy

Bureaucracy poses a never-ending challenge in most organizations. Tedious approval processes take time. Everything has to be documented. "That's not how we do things around here," usually thrusts a cog in the wheels of creativity, motivation, and progress.

There are two things you can do as a leader to clear the path.

First, you can work to increase trust. Fundamentally, excessive bureaucracy is the result of a lack of trust. Sometime, somewhere, somebody used bad judgment, and a rule was suddenly created for everyone: "You have to get two signatures on a purchase order." "You have to get your business plan signed by five different department heads." "You have to sign out for tools."

It follows that the more people can trust you, the less you'll have to worry about bureaucracy. If you are a person of unfailing integrity and reliability, the time will come when other leaders will just trust your word on things. Approvals will speed up, signatures will be easy to get, and your life will go a lot smoother. You might even be able to break down a barrier with a stroke of your pen. These things empower you as a leader to help clear the path for those you lead. Your own trustworthy character will also enable you—through example and training—to build trust and trustworthiness in your team, which further helps clear the path of restraints created by distrust.

Second, you can anticipate bureaucratic demands. You know what people need from you, so be prepared in advance. If the team complains about a procedural hang-up, ask them how it should be done differently. Have them work with you to document the problem so you can be the advocate to have it fixed. Give them templates for reporting a concern or requesting approval. Red tape is a pain, but if you've prepped your team for it, they won't be so frustrated by it.

In a Clear-the-Path Conversation about bureaucracy, you might ask questions such as these:

- ▶ "Where might we run into policy issues?"
- ▶ "Are there other ways to accomplish this goal without going up against policy?"
- ▶ "How can we improve this process?"

Budget Restraints

When team members raise budget issues, encourage creative brainstorming and focus on what you can do together. There never seems to be enough budget, so you'll want to talk about scope, timing, and alternatives. If a project threatens to overrun the budget, you may want to ask the team what ways they might see to extend the deadline or reduce the scope of the project. You might brainstorm together for hidden resources or alternative ways to meet the need. If you've been allocated a certain amount of money, explore together what you can change before you go upstairs to ask for more.

In a Clear-the-Path Conversation about budget, you might ask questions such as these:

- "Where can we change the scope of this project so we can stay within budget?"
- "Is there any flexibility on the timelines?"
- "Do we have budget elsewhere or other hidden resources we could apply here?"

Battling Objectives

Often the team runs into conflicting goals. Maybe Accounting wants to keep inventory low, but as head of the Delivery team, you're getting complaints that products are out of stock. Angry customers are demoralizing your team, so you get into a battle with the accountants, who are "obviously to blame" for the whole problem.

The fact is, both of you have reasonable goals—but your departmental goals are misaligned. Too much inventory hurts the business; so do out-of-stocks. So, what can you do to clear the path in a situation like this?

An effective solution is to hold a Clear-the-Path Conversation with people outside the team—usually peer managers. Talk about "3rd Alternatives"—not "my" solution or "your" solution, but one we come up with together that is better than what either of us could have come up with on our own.

Ask accounting for a 3rd Alternative meeting with you and a few key leaders and influencers. Share your common goals of delighting customers and increasing margins. Hear them out, and make sure you understand their position. Then ask them for the favor of hearing you (or your team member) out so everyone understands the issues on both sides. This needs to be a *conversation*, not a pitched battle among people who often have the same interest, to make sure the business succeeds.

Brainstorm together: Could there be a solution we haven't thought of before? What's actually causing out-of-stocks? Can we improve forecasting? If so, how? Do we need to share more real-time data with our customers? Is there some way we could expedite warehouse-to-location delivery of inventory? Do we need to change the timing expectation of the customer regarding fulfillment?

In a Clear-the-Path Conversation to resolve battling objectives, you might ask questions such as these:

- ▶ "What's causing this conflict in goals?"
- ▶ "What goals can we agree on?"
- ▶ "Would you be willing to look for solutions we haven't come up with yet?"

IF YOU COULD CHANGE ONE THING TO IMPROVE YOUR PROGRESS, WHAT WOULD IT BE?

When you ask people this question, often something will come up that is very doable but has just not surfaced as a point of focus. A person might say, "Well, if I could just get the shipping schedule on Friday before noon instead of on Monday morning, that would really help me plan the next week." Often the little things become big in terms of results.

On the other hand, an issue may come up that would require a lot of change, but by looking deeply into the problem, you may discover that there could be big payoffs for several people. Sticking points are often sticking points for more than one.

WHAT CAN TEAM MEMBERS DO TO REMOVE BARRIERS FOR EACH OTHER?

In reality, everyone on the team is potentially a "path clearer." We all have "Circles of Influence"—people we know and resources we have that no one else has access to. A software engineer might be able to call on a network of hundreds of other engineers for help with a knotty problem. A talented speaker on the team might be able to communicate ideas better than you can. A team member with a passion for computer games might be just the person to create a customer experience that's more fun.

In Clear-the-Path Conversations, you have the opportunity to encourage all team members to do what they can to help clear the path for others and appropriately recruit the complementary strengths of other team members to clear the path for themselves.

WHAT NEW OPPORTUNITIES ARE YOU SEEING?

One CEO in the ice cream store business would regularly ask the servers, "What are the customers saying about the flavors we offer?" This did several things. It gave them great feedback as to the market. It gave them ideas for new flavors they might create. It let the servers know they were important and that the CEO valued their observations and ability to relate with the customers. It helped the servers learn to really pay attention to the customers.

When people are encouraged to look for new opportunities, it engages them and helps clear the path for newer and better ways to accomplish desired results.

HOW CAN I BEST HELP YOU?

This question should always be asked. Without interrupting people or turning into a pest or a stalker, you should always make sure your team knows you're available to help. You'll want to make sure you stay in the role of helper, not doer.

The wording of this question is important. It's best *not* to ask, "Can I help?" Too often that question gets interpreted as, "Let me take over, and I'll tell you what to do and how to do it." Team members then get into the habit of deferring to you instead of engaging their own talents and creativity, and you end up doing their work for them. This creates a dependent culture in which team members never grow into their roles, and you find yourself turning into the typical overstressed, overburdened manager.

"How can I best help you?" is more effective. This question is always welcome. It's not a yes-or-no question; it's one that forces people to think about and be specific in their requests—even to consider if they really need your help at all. Their answer might be, "You can best help by just moving aside and letting me work on this." That's all right—you should welcome that response from a team or team member who has earned your trust. More often, the answer will be to do something only you can do—help take down a barrier, talk to an executive, or provide an approval or a resource. Teach your team to see you as the one they turn to when they really can't do something themselves.

Taking It Upstairs

When you can't clear the path with a stroke of your own pen or a conversation with peer managers, you might have to take the issue to your own leaders. Often the most important path-clearing conversations are with the people you report to.

So how do you hold a Clear-the-Path Conversation with your boss?

> Just think what it feels like in an organization when everyone knows what the real cause of the problem is but no one is willing to speak up. Of course, survival is not mandatory.
>
> —DUKE OKES

Prepare well by documenting the barrier and how it's getting in the way of your team. Include the effects in terms of costly delays, quality problems, morale issues—whatever is blocking your progress.

Find out why the barrier exists in the first place. Get a good picture of the root causes. Why is this frustrating policy in place? What's the reason for what appears to you to be an unreasonable step in a process?

Then brainstorm with your team a manageable way forward. Some organizational barriers might seem hard to get over; but remember, they are usually created internally and can be removed internally if you can make a good enough case and offer a reasonable workaround.

Finally, take your recommendation to the person or people who can do something about it. Make your case considerately but firmly.

For example, one national school system wanted to use smartphone lessons to supplement classroom learning for high school students. There were a number of barriers, but the biggest one was training all the teachers on new online-learning methods. There was no money for the training, and the teachers didn't have time for it.

The leader of the online-learning initiative brainstormed with her team to find a workaround. Finally, they came up with a solution: ask the business community for a private donation to train a handful of "early adopter" teachers who were excited to try the new curriculum. Then these early adopters would act as coaches to help other teachers gradually come on board.

The team first had to sell the government education office on the idea. It was well received, and they went on to hold meetings with potential donors. As a result, nearly every teacher in the system started using the students' own smartphones as a teaching tool, which was a huge plus for both students and teachers.

When to Hold Clear-the-Path Conversations

Ideally, Clear-the-Path Conversations follow formal Voice and Performance Conversations. With clear "voices" and Win-Win Performance Agreements in place, team members are ready to surge forward to create top performance. It's at this point that your role as a path clearer makes the biggest difference in unleashing talent.

Below are a few examples of when Clear-the-Path Conversations might arise:

▶ *Dealing with a cross-functional problem.* In a regular Performance Conversation, you might note some problems in getting the right information to the right people outside the team. You realize this is a bigger issue that affects other teams as well.

In order to clear the path, you could say, "This is a broader issue that impacts us on many levels. I'll look into it and see if I can help you get what you need. Hopefully, this will help others in the organization too."

▶ **Dealing with a breakdown.** Suppose that, in a team meeting, you discover the system for paying vendors has broken down. You realize that a call from you could likely save one of your people hours of frustrating work. You might share that information with the team and say, "Look, why don't I make that call and see what I can find out?" When you make the call, you discover there are conflicts between the goals of your team and other teams. You may determine that this issue could use some study, so you report to the team and the issue becomes an action item for your next meeting with upper management.

▶ **Clearing things up.** In several Performance Conversations, you hear different versions of the corporate goals, and you realize this is affecting sales. You make an appointment with your file leaders to get clarity around those goals so you can make sure everyone on your team knows what the goals really are.

▶ **Using your influence to help team members.** In an informal Performance Conversation, a team member says she's worried about a sudden surge in the number of customer returns. Something has evidently gone wrong with the product packaging. She's tried messaging, but nobody in that division will talk to her. You might encourage her to get more information if she can, and then you personally set up an appointment for her with the product engineer, who is often difficult to get ahold of.

▸ ***Getting approvals.*** In a Voice Conversation, a member of your team reveals she has a passion for languages and can speak several fluently. For a long time she's wanted to transfer to the translation department, but she can't get approval. So you make an appointment with the head of that department to find out what their needs are and how your team member could contribute.

Keep in mind that, just as with the other Leadership Conversations, the goal is not to simply hold a formal conversation; it's to create the environment in which informal conversations are taking place all the time. This is what effective leaders do. They learn about the capacities of their people (voice), they focus the work (performance), and then they help people accomplish their goals. Clearing the path is what good leaders do day by day, hour by hour.

For example, suppose you're in a stand-up meeting with Stan reviewing progress by the numbers. You might say something like this: "It looks like we're not where we wanted to be on this (performance). This is something we've talked about, and I know it's important to you (voice), so I know your lack of attention is not the issue. What do you think are some of the sticking points, and what can we do to improve the situation?"

As you listen, Stan shares his idea that lead-time policy may be causing at least part of the problem. You might say, "So one of the issues is Shipping's lead-time policy. Look, why don't you continue to work on the design issues, and I'll set up a meeting with Shipping to take in some of this information and see what we can do. Is there anything else you see that I could do to clear the path?"

At other times, the "right time" to hold a Clear-the-Path Conversation may surface spontaneously in the midst of a Voice or Performance Conversation.

> **AUTHOR NOTE** Once, as the manager of a new sales team, I met with each member of the team individually, getting to know them and seeking to understand where they each were in relation to their goals. One team member had been with the team for just over a year, but her production had not been impressive. She was pleasant, and was trying to put on her best face for our meeting, but it was clear she had some performance issues.
>
> As we talked, I was struck with a couple of thoughts. First, this was an impressive person. It occurred to me that if I were in the hiring process, I would recruit her to be part of this team. She was bright, personable, eager to contribute, and willing to work hard.
>
> Second, despite her willingness and capability, she simply didn't know where to begin, nor did she know what success really looked like. She had suffered through a painful first year at this company, with no vision or no direction from her manager, and felt she had been left to feel her own way in a highly ambiguous environment.
>
> As she talked, her initial good cheer quickly turned more authentic as she opened up and admitted she didn't know how to proceed. Though she was talented, she felt lost and at risk.
>
> What started as a Performance Conversation quickly became a Clear-the-Path Conversation. Together we deconstructed her expected deliverables into daily activities and reviewed how I and the other team members might be able to help. She left that conversation with clarity on how to proceed and how to get help.
>
> What followed was impressive, as she became one of the top performers on the team for the next several years. She had always had the talent to succeed. It simply needed to be unleashed, and the Clear-the-Path Conversation was the catalyst.

When Leadership Conversations are part of the culture, Clear-the-Path Conversations become a natural part of the interaction between leaders and those they lead. In fact, team members will often initiate such conversations as they learn to see your role as a "path clearer."

Where to Hold Clear-the-Path Conversations

Clearing the path happens in many different settings. It might be a formal conversation with the team covering several days. It might be a brief follow-up with a struggling team member to fulfill one part of his Win-Win Performance Agreement. Or it may be a quick "How can I best help you?" as you pass by a workstation.

Three settings that typically offer good opportunities for Clear-the-Path Conversations are teaching situations, coaching situations, and team huddles.

TEACHING SITUATIONS

Clearing the path involves more than facilitating work tasks; it often involves teaching people how to perform.

Strong leaders recognize their role as teachers and look for teaching opportunities to help team members get over the hurdles between them and success.

In one situation, for example, Sarah, a retail manager, noticed that Chad, an eager new employee, was taking very seriously the idea that he was supposed to be "available" to help customers. He was greeting every customer several times, pressing to find out what they had come in for, and basically pleading for the chance to help them. Most customers were really put off by this behavior, but Chad didn't seem to be aware. Sarah realized that she needed to help him change his idea of what it meant to be "available." She pulled him aside to teach him how to be available without being pushy.

> He who cannot change the very fabric of his thought will never be able to change reality, and will never, therefore, make any progress.
>
> —ANWAR EL-SADAT

Sarah worked with Chad for a few days, modeling how to interact with a customer, giving him quick quizzes, suggesting things to say, explaining people's need for personal space, and demonstrating how to give it to them. By doing this, she cleared the path for Chad to become a successful customer-service person.

Clearly, Sarah understood the value of her role as a teacher in clearing the path.

COACHING SITUATIONS

In today's world, the word "coaching" is not only associated with a formal role, such as that of a football or basketball coach; it is also recognized—increasingly—as one of the primary responsibilities of managers and leaders.

Often the efforts of managers to be good coaches are not very effective. Attempts to coach are perceived as efforts to control the individual or maneuvers in service of some hidden agenda. The key to avoiding perceptions such as these is trust. If those you're coaching know that you are a trustworthy person and they trust that you genuinely care about them, they see you as a source of help instead of a critic or a judge.

> **AUTHOR NOTE** I was one of several coaches for a young boys' football team for many years. I wanted to be like the coaches I had in high school and college. They believed in me. They helped me see my natural strengths

and talents, and that made all the difference. These leaders helped me understand that great things can be accomplished by working hard, competing hard, and working well as a team member.

We always reviewed six core principles before and after every practice and game. As coaches, we deeply tried to engrain these core beliefs into our kids' minds and hearts. I strongly believe that these principles helped our team compete successfully at a very high level. We would ask the boys these questions *in this order*:

1. Did you work hard and do your best?
2. Did you play as a team?
3. Did you learn something new?
4. Were you a good sport?
5. Did you have fun?
6. Did you play to win?

Over a four-year period, our record was 21 wins and 5 losses. Winning was important because it gave the kids confidence and made the games more exciting. However, "Did you play to win?" was always the last question we asked. We felt the other five questions were far more important.

As we built our team's success year after year, we tried to put each player in the best position possible for team success. We created plays and drilled the team on them. We learned from our mistakes and improved our strategies. We asked for 100 percent team commitment and disciplined practice each week. Above all, we wanted the kids to know that we cared about them individually—that we were excited about their development both on and off the field.

Parents would tell us things like this: "Our boys have loved their experience in football and now feel like they can accomplish anything. They have confidence."

In terms of process and principles, Clear-the-Path Conversations are much like good coaching. Both coaching and path clearing are cyclical. It's not "one and done," because the path doesn't stay clear—particularly if you're working to achieve measurable improvement.

> I'm very demanding about performance. I'm very demanding on myself, and I'm very demanding of the people around me. But I know that to be able to be demanding, you have to empower people. You can't be demanding of someone who isn't empowered. It isn't fair.
>
> —CARLOS GHOSN

Great coaches hold many Clear-the-Path Conversations. They "run alongside" the team. They're constantly asking team members questions and learning from them. They invite creative thinking. They give a lot of person-to-person encouragement and often remind individuals of their unique voice and the great potential of the contribution they can make. They demonstrate caring by talking about developing the "whole person"—body, heart, mind, and spirit.

According to research done by the McKinsey organization, most managers see their roles as very limited, "merely to oversee...relaying information from executives to workers. Such managers keep an eye on things, enforce plans and policies, report operational results, and quickly escalate issues or problems." As McKinsey sums it up, the typical manager's role is to "oversee, not to contribute ideas." This view of the manager's role "makes companies less productive, less agile, and less profitable."

So, what is McKinsey's solution? "To unlock a team's abilities, a manager must spend a significant amount of time on two activities: helping the team understand the company's direction and its implications for team members and *coaching for performance.* Little of either occurs on the front line today."[5]

As the McKinsey study shows, in best-practice companies, frontline managers allocate 60 to 70 percent of their time to the floor—much of it in high-quality individual coaching. The bottom-line benefit of this coaching is significant.

TEAM HUDDLES

Athletic teams often "huddle" after a play in order to take stock of the score and their situation, brainstorm how to move the score in their direction, and commit to a course of action. It all happens very quickly.

Many good business leaders "huddle" with their teams for the same reasons. They look at the score—in their case, the key measures for their goals. Where are they? Where are they supposed to be? Team members report on what seems to be working well and commit to generalize that behavior. They also report on the bumps and bottlenecks they've encountered, and they brainstorm how to clear the way forward. They look for ways to clear the path for each other. Leaders and coaches are able to hear, help, and learn.

The key to successful huddles is consistency. When held on a regular basis, they establish a cadence of accountability in the culture. Huddles become a key setting for Clear-the-Path Conversations—a place for everyone to talk about how to clear the path for everyone else instead of protecting themselves, blaming, or accusing others of poor performance.

A good way to start a huddle is by asking the team to meet and take stock of progress on team goals. Let's look at how this might play out.

YOU: "The purpose of this meeting is to touch base on our progress to see if there's anything we can do to help each other. As you can see from the scoreboard, we're not quite where we should be on moving inventory. Does anybody have any ideas as to what might be causing this situation?"

KAYLA: "Our forecasts don't seem as accurate as they should be. I'm wondering if we're getting the right point-of-sale data."

YOU: "Does anyone else see this as an issue?"

SAM: "I do. I think Kayla's right on."

MIKA: "I have a question. Do you think the employees at point-of-sale are actually using the equipment right? Maybe we should do a little more training."

THEO: "I think we're giving the inventory people too much leeway. We've told them 10 percent, plus or minus, is okay, so they might be sloppy with their estimates. We could tighten it up to 5 percent."

YOU: "These are both great ideas. Mika, what would you like to do?"

MIKA: "I can go check on the curriculum and make sure we're training people correctly on the equipment."

GEORGE: "I have access to the training materials. I can send everything to Mika, and I'd be glad to help her update them."

YOU: "Super. And Theo?"

THEO: "Let me run the figures and see if a change in the inventory leeway would make a difference that's worth anything. But you'll need to clear the path for me to actually ask people to tighten up."

YOU: "I'll have a talk with the floor manager and make sure that happens."

A huddle should be brief, focused on the goals and measures, and centered on how team members can clear the path for each other. You don't want to make it a long, drawn-out complaint session; in fact, the best huddles are often stand-up meetings that take only a few minutes. Notice also that the leader gives little direction—it's the team members who raise issues and make commitments to solve them.

Huddles are called for the specific purpose of clearing the path. But you can have Clear-the-Path Conversations anywhere—in staff meetings, retreats, conferences...anywhere you need to discuss progress on goals and how to help each other move forward. The focus is always on improvement. The conversation can be very short or it can be more involved if a key opportunity or an obstacle comes along.

Furthermore, anyone can initiate or even lead a huddle. As a leader, you want the team to develop a proactive approach to achieving the goals. By rotating responsibility for the huddle, you can help team members take ownership for the goals and their own creative solutions to problems that come up.

There are many opportunities to hold Clear-the-Path Conversations. Although leaders shouldn't be hovering and interrupting all the time, many err in the other direction—they don't hold these conversations often enough. In fact, the evidence shows that leader feedback is downright rare: Dartmouth's Sydney Finkelstein reports, "Only 2 percent of managers provide ongoing feedback to their employees. Just 2 percent!"[6] With Clear-the-Path Conversations, we don't have to be like the majority of leaders who neglect such important communication.

Clear-the-Path Conversations: Watchouts

As with Voice and Performance Conversations, there are important watchouts for leaders in holding Clear-the-Path Conversations. (See Figure 4.5.) Three of the most important attitudes for leaders to avoid are listed, as follows.

FIGURE 4.5

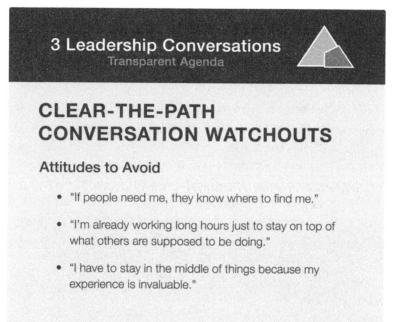

3 Leadership Conversations
Transparent Agenda

CLEAR-THE-PATH CONVERSATION WATCHOUTS

Attitudes to Avoid

- "If people need me, they know where to find me."

- "I'm already working long hours just to stay on top of what others are supposed to be doing."

- "I have to stay in the middle of things because my experience is invaluable."

▶ *"You know where to find me."* This attitude produces endless missed opportunities. Team members hesitate to approach you. They don't see you much. They get the impression you're too important to be disturbed. But if you go to them and initiate conversations with them, they get to know you better and feel more comfortable with you. And if you invite them to tell you about their issues and concerns, you'll know what you need to know. It's tempting to stay in your own space and work on your own stuff—*but that's not your job as a leader.*

▶ ***"I'm doing enough as it is."*** You want to avoid giving this impression: "I'm already working long hours to stay on top of what others are supposed to be doing." Obviously, nobody will want to "bother" you because you've already labeled him or her as a nuisance. No real leader ever puts the team off this way.

▶ ***"I've got all the answers."*** You also don't want to see yourself (or encourage others to see you) as the fount of all knowledge, all solutions, all wisdom. You're not. Nobody is. Good ideas can come from anywhere, anytime. Clearing the path does not require you to think of everything and fix everything. It won't work, and besides, you'll never last. On the contrary, clearing the path is everybody's job. Your task is to recruit everyone to do that job.

Final Words

When we do research on an organization, we ask people to respond "yes" or "no" to this question: "Does the following statement describe you?"

I have a leader who is helpful to me
in accomplishing my work.

We have found a significant correlation between positive answers to that question and organizational performance. In personal interviews with team members, we've had energetic discussions about all the ways people feel their leaders help them. You can feel the energy in a high-performing organization.

On the other hand, in low-performing organizations, the question typically evokes sarcasm: "Yeah, I suppose if you think that piling it on and tightening the screws is helpful!"

Or, "What leader? I haven't seen her in six months." When interviewing bosses about these responses, we often hear comments such as, "Sure, I'd like to spend more time coaching and mentoring, but the practical reality is that I just don't have time."

Why don't these bosses feel like they have time? Because their idea of leadership is moving information up and down, micromanaging, postponing, and helicoptering anxiously from one crisis to another. Or they see leadership with some skewed notion of "empowerment"—they think they're empowering team members when the reality is they're simply abandoning them. Bottom line, these managers and leaders are not removing obstacles; they're creating them. They're obscuring the path—not clearing it—and low performance is the result.

Clear-the-Path Conversations are the final leg of the three-legged stool in high-performing organizations. They communicate caring: "One of my most important jobs as a leader is to help clear the path so that you can do your job. I value discussion that helps me know what's getting in your way and what I—or we together—can do to remove the obstacles."

When team members feel their voice and contribution are respected, when expectations are clear, and when paths are cleared of obstacles, then talent can be fully unleashed. As a leader, you can focus energy on the most important wins for the organization, the team, and the individual. You free up the team to succeed.

DISCUSSION QUESTIONS

1. How would you define Clear-the-Path Conversations?
2. Why do Clear-the-Path Conversations generally come after the formal Voice and Performance Conversations?
3. What kind of character traits can enable you to hold more effective Clear-the-Path Conversations? How important do you believe qualities such as honesty, trustworthiness, and keeping your commitments are to the process?
4. How would you describe the mindset of a leader who effectively clears the path?
5. How would you find the time to clear the path for others?
6. How would you measure the performance of a leader who does a lot of "path clearing"?
7. What are the costs of failure to clear the path for the team?
8. What are some opportunities in your work for holding Clear-the-Path Conversations?
9. Why is it vital for everyone on the team to learn how to clear the path? How can you engage team members in clearing the path for others?
10. What do you think is the difference between clearing the path and micromanaging?
11. What steps would be important for you to take before you direct a problem to your own leaders?
12. How could you help your own leaders do more "path clearing" for you?

CHAPTER 5

FOUR UNLEASHING PRINCIPLES

The habit of the active utilization of well-understood princi-
ples is the final possession of wisdom.

—ALFRED NORTH WHITEHEAD

The Bricklayer's Story

Dear Sir,

I am writing in response to your request for additional
information in Block #3 of the accident reporting form. I put
"Poor Planning" as the cause of my accident. You asked for
a fuller explanation and I trust the following details will be
sufficient.

I am a bricklayer by trade. On the day of the accident, I was
working alone on the roof of a new six-story building. When I
completed my work, I found I had some bricks left over which,
when weighed later, were found to weigh 240 lbs. Rather than
carry the bricks down by hand, I decided to lower them in a
barrel by using a pulley which was attached to the side of the
building at the sixth floor.

Securing the rope at ground level, I went up to the roof, swung the barrel out and loaded the bricks into it. Then I went down and untied the rope, holding it tightly to ensure a slow descent of the 240 lbs. of bricks. You will note on the accident reporting form that my weight is 135 lbs. Due to my surprise at being jerked off the ground so suddenly, I lost my presence of mind and forgot to let go of the rope. Needless to say, I pro-ceeded at a rapid rate up the side of the building.

In the vicinity of the third floor, I met the barrel, which was now proceeding downward at an equally impressive speed. This explains the fractured skull, minor abrasions, and the broken collarbone, as listed in Section 3, accident reporting form. Slowed only slightly, I continued my rapid ascent, not stopping until the fingers of my right hand were two knuckles deep into the pulley which I mentioned in Paragraph 2 of this correspon-dence. Fortunately, by this time I had regained my presence of mind and was able to hold tightly to the rope, in spite of the excruciating pain I was now beginning to experience.

At approximately the same time, however, the barrel of bricks hit the ground and the bottom fell out of the barrel. Now devoid of the weight of the bricks, the barrel weighed approx-imately 50 lbs. I refer you again to my weight. As you might imagine, I began a rapid descent down the side of the building. In the vicinity of the third floor, I met the barrel coming up. This accounts for the two fractured ankles, broken tooth, and severe lacerations of my legs and lower body.

Here my luck began to change slightly. The encounter with the barrel seemed to slow me enough to lessen my injuries when I fell into the pile of bricks and fortunately only three vertebrae were cracked.

I am sorry to report, however, as I lay there on the pile of bricks, in pain, unable to move and watching the empty barrel six stories above me, I again lost my composure and presence of mind and let go of the rope. And I lay there watching the empty barrel begin its journey back onto me.[1]

This is a great example of the consequence of neglecting a natural law, or principle—in this case, the principle of gravity. A principle is a self-evident truth that never changes. We might choose to ignore the existence of a principle. But as the story points out, we will most certainly suffer the consequences if we do.

Just as there are principles such as gravity that govern in the natural world, there are also principles such as honesty, integrity, and patience that govern in human interactions. For example, if we are honest, we will build trust. If we are dishonest, it will lead to suspicion and distrust. This principle of honesty is universally applicable in both work and personal life. We can respect these principles, or we can ignore them; but the quality of our lives, relationships, and leadership depends on the degree to which we choose to understand and align our lives with these unchanging, universal truths.

The 3 Leadership Conversations in this book are based on timeless principles of effectiveness in human interaction. In this chapter, we'd like to explore four of the fundamental principles that are at the very core of the content and process of the conversations. We'd like to look at how you, as a leader, can nurture these principles in your own life and in the lives of those you lead.

Principle 1: Contribution

In 1776, Scottish economist and moral philosopher Adam Smith wrote *The Wealth of Nations*, which today is considered a fundamental work in classical economics. In the minds of some, Smith's theory was that if everyone works for his or her own self-interest, the economy will flourish; that at the end of the day, "winning" at almost any cost is the essence of the free-enterprise system and is good for all; and that it is the "invisible hand" of the marketplace that makes us all prosper.

But this is not what Adam Smith taught. Without going into a lengthy discussion of his theories of economics, let's just remember that he was a professor of moral philosophy. His main point was that business works *when people have what he called "intentional virtue."* People can look to their own self-interest; but for an economy to work, it must not be at the expense of others through cheating or manipulation. A society will prosper only to the extent that this "intentional virtue" and moral character abound.

In *A Theory of Moral Sentiments*, Smith said:

> It is not the love of our neighbor, it is not the love of mankind, which upon many occasions prompts us to the practice of those divine virtues. It is a stronger love, a more powerful affection, which generally takes place upon such occasions: the love of what is honorable and noble, of the grandeur, and dignity, and superiority of our own characters.[2]

If you want to have a top-performing team, you want to nurture in the members of that team that "stronger love" of the principles that create "intentional virtue"—particularly the principle of contribution. You want to help them understand that making the contribution they feel they should make is a matter of personal honor and integrity. If you have people on your team who are morally bankrupt, no "invisible hand" will keep them from cheating and bringing everyone down. The various financial crises we've all lived through provide ample evidence of that.

People with "intentional virtue" tend to be contributors rather than consumers. They operate out of a different paradigm. Where consumers see the world in terms of taking, contributors see the world in terms of giving. Where consumption creates fear and scarcity of resources, contribution generates hope and expands opportunity.

> The heart of global citizenship is about ethics and conduct. It begins with the way a company thinks about its role in the world. Does it simply exist to make as much money as possible?
>
> —DEBORAH DUNN

With a contribution paradigm, the basic economic transaction is the win-win exchange of goods and services. A "better deal" always *gives* value. It's a creating paradigm.

With the consumption paradigm, the basic transaction is simply, "I win—and it really doesn't matter what happens to you in the process." The "better deal" is not the one that *gives* value, it's one that *takes* value from you for my benefit. It produces false wealth because nothing new is created except resentment. Taken to the extreme, this is the paradigm of the dictator who amasses great personal wealth and leaves an impoverished country in his wake.

As we've seen, this mindset among certain big economic players can lead to disaster. In the midst of the 2008 recession, it forced U.S. Federal Reserve Chairman Alan Greenspan to admit "that he had put too much faith in the self-correcting power of free markets and had failed to anticipate the self-destructive power of wanton mortgage lending." In his words, "Those of us who have looked to the self-interest of lending institutions to protect shareholders' equity, myself included, are in a state of shocked disbelief."[3]

In his best-selling book *The Ultimate Question*, Fred Reichheld explains the difference in results between the paradigms of contribution and consumption in terms of "good and bad profits." According to him:

> While bad profits don't show up on the books, they are easy to recognize. Whenever a customer [and we would add, an employee] feels misled, mistreated, ignored, or coerced, then profits from that customer are bad. Bad profits come from unfair or misleading pricing or disadvantage. Bad profits arise when companies seek to save money by delivering a lousy customer [or employee] experience or from a misaligned policy that is unjust or unfair. Bad profits are *about extracting the maximum value from customers, not in creating value.*[4]

Good profits, he says, come from delighted customers and employees who feel the organization is really contributing to their well-being. For example, Amazon invests heavily in making the customer experience as easy as possible. Costco invests in the team, paying them much more than market rates and thus attracting a class of employees who give excellent service. Disney provides a remarkable experience not only for customers, but also for "cast members"—their term for employees. These wildly profitable companies are certainly not perfect, but they prosper and show the benefits of a culture of contribution.

As we think about this principle with regard to the 3 Leadership Conversations, we can see that it applies in all three areas—voice, performance, and clearing the path. But we'd like to focus on how it is particularly center stage to the Voice Conversation.

As we've said, the whole purpose of "finding your voice" is to define the unique contribution that is yours to make. It's the principle of sharing the best you have to offer, making the difference you want to make, and leaving the legacy you want to leave. It's the spirit of contribution in voice that unleashes your talents, passion, and highest values.

This is vitally important to you, personally, as a leader, and also to those you lead. So how do you go about it?

You can live it. When you base your own leadership voice on the principle of contribution, you unleash your talents and abilities in a way that *contributes* to the purposes and goals of your organization and to society

> Simply focusing on money in and of itself is an empty goal. I find the rich much poorer. Sometimes they are more lonely inside. They are never satisfied. They always need something more.
>
> —MOTHER TERESA

as a whole. Not only does this enrich your own life; it also sets a powerful example for those you lead, encouraging them to do the same.

You can look for it. You can celebrate contribution in team members. You can recognize the difference it makes when people are motivated by it. You can look for people who value contribution as you make new hires.

You can teach it. In your training and in your Voice Conversations particularly, you can help people connect with the principle and spirit of contribution.

As you help people connect with voice, some may feel that contribution is not really "their thing" or that they can contribute better in another role on another team. That's okay; in fact, it's probably best for you both to find out sooner than later.

Others may feel that they can best contribute in a different role within the team, and you can work together to figure out ways to restructure in order to best maximize that contribution.

Others may not initially see their job in terms of "contribution." As you teach them the importance of the principle, you may be able to help them connect with their role in a new way.

Perhaps you're familiar with the story of the priest in Italy who comes up to three stonecutters working in the hot afternoon sun. He asks the first, "My son, what are you doing?"

The man replies, "I am cutting stone."

The priest then asks the second man, "What are you doing?" The stonecutter replies, "I'm making 100 lira a day."

Finally, he asks the third stonecutter the same question. This worker replies, "I am building a beautiful cathedral."

As a leader, you can help team members reframe the way they see what they do. Even if a person is working primarily to provide for a family, that person will find more joy and engagement in the job if he or she recognizes that providing for a family is also a valuable contribution.

In preparing for Voice Conversations with the principle of contribution in mind, it may be helpful to ask yourself questions such as these:

- ▶ Am I motivated by a sense of contribution in my work? Do I communicate my passion and excitement about contribution to those I lead?
- ▶ Do I sometimes switch to being more of a consumer than a contributor? How does that affect my view of others? How does that affect my influence on others?
- ▶ Which team members tend to be "consumers" and which tend to be "contributors"? How can I help the "consumers" change the way they see their work?
- ▶ What contributions do we need from each person on the team?
- ▶ How can we orchestrate the contribution of each person for the benefit of all?

More and more, enlightened leaders are focusing on contribution because it's becoming clear that not only is it good business, it literally changes our view of the world from one of scarcity—where everyone's fighting for the crumbs—to one of abundance, where, if we all work with "intentional virtue," there's enough for everybody to win.

Principle 2: Trust

Like contribution, the principle of trust is integral to each of the Leadership Conversations. But here we'd like to focus on the vital nature of trust in the Performance Conversation. Creating Win-Win Performance Agreements and working together as a team to accomplish important goals both require that people trust each other. When you trust the members of your team, you set them free to perform with excellence—to do their best work in their best way.

For some people, trusting is hard. As the research shows, trust today is at a historic low in nearly every institution you can name—financial markets, business, commerce, government, education, and religious organizations. And we all pay a big price for that.

Business scholar Francis Fukuyama has said, "Widespread distrust in a society imposes a kind of tax on all forms of economic activity, a tax that high-trust societies do not have to pay."[5] When leaders operate in a low-trust way, "Trust Taxes" accrue in the form of stagnation and cynicism.

As Stephen M. R. Covey explains in his landmark best-selling book *The Speed of Trust,* trust is more than just a nice social virtue, it has very measurable, practical business consequences. When trust goes up, the speed of business goes up and costs go down. When trust goes down, speed also goes down while costs increase. These are the "Trust Taxes" we all pay.

Clearly, the more we can build trust in our teams and organizations, the more we can turn taxes into dividends—not only the financial dividends of working better together to accomplish important goals, but also the social dividends of enjoying high-trust relationships in our work.

> One who doesn't really trust himself can never really trust anyone else.
>
> —JEAN-FRANÇOIS DE GONDI

Covey lists 13 Behaviors that help develop trust. Although all 13 apply, some are particularly high-leverage in conducting Performance Conversations, both with individuals and with the team. As you prepare for Performance Conversations, you may want to evaluate how well you demonstrate these important trust-building behaviors:

- **Talk Straight.** Are you truthful about guidelines and resources? Do you overpromise resources? Do you impose unreasonable guidelines because you're under pressure from above? Are you honest about the agenda that is driving you? Are you straightforward about company politics?

- **Clarify Expectations.** Do all team members understand what you expect of them and what they should expect of you, or is there a chance you may surprise them later by changing your tune?

- **Hold Yourself and Others Accountable for Commitments.** (This is actually a combination of two of the behaviors.) Do you always honor your commitments and expect others to honor theirs, or do you let commitments slide, make excuses for yourself or others, or forget you even made a commitment? Do you hold everyone to the same standard of accountability, or do you "tell off" some people but not others when they don't follow through?

▶ **Deliver Results.** Do you always deliver on the commitments you make, or are you long on talk but short on delivery? Are you extremely "busy," but ineffective and unproductive? Can your team count on you to come through for them?

As you might imagine, these behaviors have a significant impact in creating high-trust relationships and high-trust outcomes for the team. One of the great benefits of Leadership Conversations is the opportunities they provide for you to demonstrate these high-trust behaviors in a practical context. If you make a point of modeling these behaviors as you converse, you build a trusting relationship with the team.

Take a look at more of the trust-building behaviors. As you do, think about some of the questions you might ask yourself regarding each. Also, think about the results your answers are creating in terms of individual and team performance.[*]

- ▶ Demonstrate Respect
- ▶ Create Transparency
- ▶ Right Wrongs
- ▶ Show Loyalty
- ▶ Get Better
- ▶ Confront Reality
- ▶ Listen First
- ▶ Extend Trust

---

[*] For a more complete exploration of each of these behaviors, refer to *The Speed of Trust* by Stephen M. R. Covey.

This last behavior, "Extend Trust," is particularly important in working with teams. But some leaders find this very hard to do—sometimes because of the high standards they set for their own performance.

Nevertheless, extending trust is fundamental to unleashing capacity. You can't "let go" or release people to fully engage their talents and act without your supervision unless you're willing to trust them.

Following are some examples of ways you can extend trust in a Performance Conversation. Notice how extending trust often builds trust on multiple levels.

> ▸ You're discussing desired results. You genuinely try to understand how the other person sees the priorities, but it's hard. She ranks the projects almost opposite from the way you do. But instead of just "telling her the way it is," you try to really listen and see things from her point of view. You listen with the intent to understand, not to reply. In this way, you demonstrate trust in her and in her knowledge, experience, and ability. In the process, you may gain more context and data from her perspective. In fact, you may even learn that she has some awareness of customer needs that you don't have and be glad you listened. But even if you find you still disagree on priorities and you need to work together to find a 3rd Alternative solution, as a result of the conversation, she will be lifted by your trust, and your trust in her as a valued team member will increase. And it will be much easier for the two of you to discover 3rd Alternatives, both now and in the future.
>
> ▸ A team member asks you to reconsider the scope of a project you're assigning to him. He doesn't feel qualified to do some of the things you've asked him to do.

So you work at carefully defining expectations. You communicate your trust in him and in his ability to carry out this assignment. Because part of your goal is to grow this team member's capacity, you ask him to stretch a little bit, but you ensure him that you'll be available to help by clearing the path. As he trusts the confidence you have in him and moves ahead, and as you follow through in your commitment to help clear the path, his trust in you, your judgment, and your integrity grows—as does both his trust and yours in his ability to perform with excellence.

> To trust life, you have to trust others; and to trust others, you have to trust yourself.
>
> —The *Bhagavad Gita*

▶ As you engage in a Performance Conversation with one team member, she starts talking about the failure of another team member to do his part on the job. You simply say, "Let's get him on the phone and see what light he can shed on the subject." In other words, you don't let the conversation turn into a blaming, finger-pointing session about someone who's not there. You make sure to understand the whole story before you start holding people accountable unfairly. This action builds trust not only in your relationship with the person who's being accused, but also in your relationship with the person who did the accusing. Consciously or subconsciously, she gets the feeling that, in a different conversation, if someone were to bring up an issue about her, you could be trusted to ensure that she would not be unfairly accused.

One of the dangers of neglecting Performance Conversations is a loss of trust. Things start to slip. We forget to keep commitments. We might start "spinning" or trying to talk ourselves out of problems we've created, pleading that the expectations weren't "clear." We might be tempted to deliver something other than what we promised to deliver. Taken together, this pattern of behavior erodes trust in a relationship.

There are also other things that damage or even destroy trust. Performance Conversations provide good opportunities to redeem and rebuild. You can hold these conversations more often, and in them, you can work hard to demonstrate some of the trust-building behaviors we've talked about, such as clarifying expectations, talking straight, making and keeping commitments, and delivering results. Over time, these behaviors can make a huge positive difference when people don't trust each other to perform. In a way, these behaviors *define* performance.

In restoring trust, it's up to you to lead the way—even in the "little" things. For example, suppose you're talking with a team member and you unintentionally "blow off" a comment she makes. When you later realize what you've done, you can take a few minutes to go to her and confidentially and personally apologize. In doing so, you communicate to her that her feelings are important to you. In righting that wrong, you're taking action to restore trust.

Being trusted grows out of being trustworthy. Most people think they are trustworthy—but unfortunately, we all tend to judge ourselves based on our intent while others judge us based on our behavior. And sometimes there's a gap between our intent and the way we behave.

In order to communicate trustworthiness to others, we need to model both good intent and effective behaviors—and we need to course-correct quickly when we don't. As Stephen

R. Covey has written: "You can't talk you way out of a problem that you have behaved yourself into." As his son Stephen M. R. Covey added, "No, but you can *behave* yourself out of problems you've behaved yourself into—and often faster than you think!" The more we demonstrate trustworthiness through our behavior, the more people will come to feel that we should be trusted.

Clearly, both building and rebuilding trust begins with you. The more you demonstrate your own trustworthiness, the more you inspire others to be trustworthy. The more you extend trust to others, the more they will extend trust to you and to others on the team. The more you create trust in the environment, the more people will feel free to unleash their talents and work together to accomplish important goals. The more you lead your team in restoring trust when it's been broken, the more people will gain trust in your commitment to the principle and your willingness to do what it takes to ensure that it's honored.

Leadership conversations provide natural opportunities to build the kind of trusted relationships you want to have with the people on your team. They also allow you to do a running audit of the "Trust Accounts" you have with your co-workers. As you interact, you can assess the balance in each account and look for high-leverage ways to increase it.

Principle 3: Synergy

Synergy is what happens when the whole is greater than the sum of the parts: in other words, 1 + 1 = 3—or more. To illustrate, consider the question, "How many pounds can a draft horse pull?" Answer: About 1,000 pounds. "How many pounds can two draft horses pull?" Answer: About 4,000 pounds. In this case, 1 + 1 = 4. Why this result? By pulling together, each horse compensates for the other's weakness. They complement each other; they fill in performance gaps. Each horse is powerful on its own, but together, their strength is remarkable!

To one degree or another, most of us have experienced synergy. Have you ever been a member of a great team? Have you found that working with certain people leads you both to be more creative than you could be by yourself?

In teams and organizations, synergy is what we reach for. It's embodied in the saying, "We're better together than we are alone."

If effectively conducted, all 3 Leadership Conversations nurture synergy. But it's really central to Clear-the-Path Conversations. When you're up against an obstacle, when you're trying to achieve a goal you've never achieved before, you need to be able to bring people with diverse strengths together to create ways to remove barriers and clear the path for each other.

Years ago, people were frustrated with Internet search engines. They were awkward to use, and it was very difficult for people to find what they were looking for. They were basically just repositories for huge quantities of unsorted information.

It took a synergistic team of two very different people to break through that barrier. Sergey Brin and Larry Page were computer-science students when they met in college. They didn't even like each other. "We were both obnoxious," Sergey recalls. Whatever Sergey said, Larry would contradict, and then Sergey would automatically come right back at him. Eventually, they realized it was fun playing this game, and they became friends.

Still, in almost every way, they were opposites. Sergey was wild, determined to be rich, and loved parties. Larry was an introvert who was focused on mathematics and didn't care about much else.

Partly due to Sergey's insatiable desire for knowledge, they started experimenting with different ways to search the Internet. Larry came up with the idea of finding information by counting how often other people looked for it. He figured the more clicks, the more important the information. His strength in math enabled him to create the complex algorithms necessary. So Larry and Sergey came up with a revolutionary new way for people to find exactly what they wanted on the Internet.

> Power can be seen as power with rather than power over, and it can be used for competence and cooperation, rather than dominance and control.
>
> —ANNE L. BARSTOW

Separately, Sergey and Larry were just a couple of bright guys who agreed on virtually nothing and had opposite personalities. Together, however, their synergy was astounding. By combining their strengths, they created a great service and a great company we now call Google. Neither could have done it alone.[6]

Let's look at a few of the attitudes typically shared by people who value the principle of synergy and enjoy the benefits.

THEY THINK WIN-WIN

This means they care about others' wins as well as their own.

In the interviews we held as part of our research for this book, we asked people to rate themselves on a scale of 1 to 5 regarding this statement:

"My teammates and I care as much about each other's success as we do about our own."

There was an almost perfect correlation between those who responded with a "5" ("This statement describes me very well") and those who loved their work. The willingness to clear the path so everyone can move forward to accomplish goals is essential to a great team.

THEY VALUE DIFFERENCES

They're not threatened by diversity in thinking style, knowledge, personality, ethnicity, gender, or other factors. In fact, they welcome diversity. Instead of saying, "You think differently—you're either crazy or wrong," they say, "You think differently—I need to listen to you."

Valuing differences means that rather than taking the same old pathways, people work together to create *new* and *better* pathways. This is synergy in action: the results of collaboration exceed the sum of the results of the individual inputs.

THEY LIKE NEW AND BETTER IDEAS

They don't give up easily and they're always looking for a better way. If one path looks blocked, they'll create another. If a barrier looks insurmountable, they just take it as a challenge to surmount it rather than backing off in discouragement. If you unleash them, they'll break through. This is the spirit of "clear the path."

People who Think Win-Win, who value different thinking, and who love trying out new ideas—these are the people you want on your team, clearing the path for each other. And of course, you must be one of them. So use the Clear-the-Path Conversations to help both you and members of your team develop those attitudes. Remember, it all starts with you.

Principle 4: Empathy

In all 3 Leadership Conversations, one of the most important things we can do as leaders, coaches, and mentors is to listen—*really* listen—with empathy. Many of us are so caught up in our own agendas, schedules, and challenges that we don't even think about the value of simply listening to *understand*, with no intent to judge, criticize, editorialize, prepare a response, probe, or share our own autobiography... just to really, genuinely, deeply hear another human being and comprehend what that person is saying.

To listen with empathy is one of the greatest manifestations of truly caring. It demonstrates respect for someone. It says, "I value you. I value your uniqueness, your thoughts, your ideas, and your experience. I value what you bring to this conversation, what you bring to this team and this organization, and I value what I can learn from you." It creates a situation in which people feel safe to express their thoughts, feelings, and ideas—to take risks and to give their best without fear of censure or ridicule.

Although there are things we can learn that will help us listen better, listening with empathy is fundamentally a heart-set and mindset. If the deep desire to genuinely understand another human being is not there, no amount of skill in "active listening" or any other technique will communicate the caring that is absolutely foundational to the principle of empathy. In fact, most often it will cause people to feel that they are being manipulated and will become counterproductive. When there is a foundation of genuine caring, however, there are things we can learn that will help us communicate that caring more effectively.[7]

For leaders to listen with real empathy is absolutely fundamental to igniting potential and unleashing talent. Not

> Next to physical survival, the greatest need of a human being is psychological survival—to be understood, to be affirmed, to be validated, to be appreciated. When you listen with empathy to another person, you give that person psychological air. And after that vital need is met, you can then focus on influencing or problem solving. This need for psychological air impacts communication in every area of life.
>
> —STEPHEN R. COVEY

only does it benefit the individual and the team or organization; it also benefits you as a leader or a coach. As people feel comfortable in expressing their thoughts and feelings, you'll find you will get more accurate information and insight for decision making, and increasingly, people will begin to work out their problems on their own.

An associate of ours shared a tender experience she had in listening with empathy:

A couple of years ago, I spent some time really focused on being a better listener and generally improving my listening skills. This was often a challenge for me, since I tend to want to move quickly and just get things done.

In the midst of my effort to improve in this area, my mother suffered a major heart attack. She had already had two major surgeries in the preceding nine months, and now faced another one—a triple bypass. As we talked, she told me that she didn't want any more surgeries and felt that she would rather let nature take its course than go through another major surgical procedure with another potentially long and difficult recovery.

My natural tendency was to jump in and try and fix the problem for her. The best path seemed very clear to me. I wanted to tell her that, yes, a triple bypass was difficult, but within just a short period of time, she would feel remarkably better. I wanted to share with her the data I found on the Internet that showed how successful this kind of surgery was and what other people her age had experienced. I was ready with a recovery plan that highlighted how all of her children—myself included—would care for her during that time, what respite options she had, and how quickly it could all be done. I had a wonderful plan, and all I had to do was get her on board with it.

But thankfully, before I got those words out of my mouth, I stopped and reminded myself that she had every right to be treated the way she wanted to be treated—or not. Her life decisions were hers, not mine, no matter how much I might like things to be different. I also realized that she was physically and emotionally exhausted. What she needed was a safe situation in which she could think through and make her own decisions. She didn't need someone to challenge or instruct her; she only needed someone to love and understand her.

So as she expressed her feelings, I simply reflected back to her the words, thoughts, feelings, and pain she expressed— both verbally and nonverbally. I didn't try to advise or correct or motivate her; I simply empathized and listened.

Again, she told me she was overwhelmed and she didn't want any more surgeries. We shed some tears together. I assured her of my love for her and told her that whatever she chose, I would fully support.

We sat for a while in silence. The lovely feeling of peace came into the room. She said, "You know, I really would like to see the grandkids grow up."

"I know they'd love to have you around," I replied.

Finally, she added, "Perhaps I could do this one more time. Could you be there with me?"

Mom went on to have the surgery and made a full recovery, and two years later, she is doing very well. But it could also have gone the other way. What really mattered was that she had the psychological space to express her feelings and to feel understood.

Once she had that, she could go to the next level of seeing what she really wanted in the long term—more time with her grandchildren. She knew the decision was hers, and either way, it was okay for her to choose the one she really wanted.

Something special happens when we really listen to another human being. Often, people don't even know what they want because they've never been allowed to fully explore what they want or how they feel. Too often they end up defending their position or fighting for air time.

But when we allow others to solve their own problems and ask for what they really want, not only are they able to get to the bottom of what they truly desire, think, and feel, but we, as leaders, become better, more informed people who are often changed in the process. And that is how we begin to truly unleash what is possible.

AUTHOR NOTE One of the most dramatic demonstrations of the power of empathy I've ever seen was when I participated in a program in South Africa shortly after the release of President Nelson Mandela after his having spent 27 years in prison. Following years of apartheid and civil unrest, South Africa's first multiracial elections were held. Invited to the program were 45 government, business, and education leaders, as well as anti-apartheid leaders—some of whom had also recently been released from prison. The purpose of the three-day event was to try to help these leaders understand each other's points of view and to learn to work together.

Clearly, it was a bold undertaking, as some of the participants had been on opposite sides of a wide chasm of social and political separation for years and had paradigms and feelings that, in some cases, were intense and diametrically opposed. Nevertheless, they all expressed their willingness to see if they could make this new government work.

As the program began and these people sat down across from each other, there was an almost tangible underlying tension. After a time, however, the power of some of the timeless principles being discussed began to lessen a measure of the anxiety.

The real breakthrough came on the second day as the discussion and activities focused on Habit 5: Seek First to Understand, Then to Be Understood. Practicing the principles and skills they'd just been taught, the participants eventually began to actually listen to each other with some degree of empathy—genuinely seeking to understand. As a result, people slowly began to open up, to share some of their deeper thoughts and experiences. And as those on one side of the fence, so to speak, were able to see and understand something of how those on the other side thought and felt and what they had been through, a deep sense of respect gradually began to replace the tension.

This opening up led to a powerful closing event the following night under the starry South African sky. We all had dinner together around a campfire in a *boma* (an area surrounded by a tall bamboo enclosure to keep the lions and other predators out). Afterward we ate and had a sharing time where people expressed their feelings about the experiences of the past few days.

Then the Shangaan women came out and sang and danced. After a few minutes, two of the program participants got up and joined in the singing and dancing. Then they motioned for others to also join, and soon everyone—South Africans of Afrikaner and British descent, Americans, game rangers, black, white, old, young, aristocrats, and ex-convicts—all were singing and dancing around the fire in a joyous celebration of unity and synergy. The lodge staff later expressed their amazement and said that in the 31 years of the resort's history, they had never seen anything like it. It was a joyful, humbling experience to be part of.

Real listening doesn't necessarily happen only in deep personal interactions or face-to-face conversations. With the genuine desire to understand, even simple interactions can provide the opportunity to listen with empathy. (See Figure 5.1.)

FIGURE 5.1

3 Leadership Conversations
Transparent Agenda

FOUR GOVERNING PRINCIPLES

Principle 1: Contribution

- Make a positive difference.
- Add value.

OPPOSITE: Greed, apathy, selfishness

Principle 2: Trust

- Be trustworthy.
- Make and keep commitments.

OPPOSITE: Distrust, suspicion, cynicism

Principle 3: Synergy

- Merge differences in unity of purpose to create a power greater than the sum of the parts.

OPPOSITE: Scarcity

Principle 4: Empathy

- Listen to genuinely understand.

OPPOSITE: Listen with intent to judge, criticize, editoralize, prepare a response, or share your own autobiography.

3 Leadership Conversations
Transparent Agenda

REMINDERS

- You are having conversations all the time—intentional or unintentional, formal, or informal. Make sure you are communicating what you want to communicate.

- Everyone has potential for extraordinary contribution. Make sure you "see" the people you work with as expanding, growing contributors with unique and extraordinary contributions to make.

OPPORTUNITIES

- You observe a team member who does not seem enthused about work or who doubts his or her ability. This is your chance to have a meaningful "Voice Conversation."

- You observe an individual or team that seems to be working hard but not really achieving meaningful results. This is your chance to have a quality "Performance Conversation."

- You see your team working hard, but you want to facilitate greater results. This is you opportunity to have a helpful "Clear-the-Path Conversation."

One co-worker said:

I was working with a group of young people one day, and we were learning about the importance of listening empathically. We had several rounds of practice with the skill face to face, and then we set the challenge to go home and have an empathic conversation.

The next morning the team came back and shared their results. One of the group, a part-time employee and college student, related that he had been texting a friend the night before. He asked her how work had been, and she said she'd had a rough day. He was about to tell her his day was pretty fun, when he realized that he had an opportunity to be in the moment with her and practice better listening.

So instead, he simply texted back, "Sounds like your day was tough." There was no judgement or analysis—just a simple restatement of what she had shared to show that he was listening and interested.

What came back really surprised him. "She sent me five more texts telling me all about what had happened. And the final one said, 'Thanks for letting me vent. You're a great friend!'"

He was amazed. All he had done was give her an affirmation, via a short, simple text, that he was interested in the fact that she had had a bad day.

How Leadership Conversations Impact Organizational Culture—and Why It Matters

Years ago, organizational behavior Professor J. Bonner Ritchie wrote a humorous story that demonstrates, among other things, how conversation affects the culture of an organization.

Though the story itself is somewhat dated, the principle is timeless and is applicable even in today's world.

"How's it going down there?" barked the big walrus from his perch on the big rock near the shore. He waited for the good word. Down below, the smaller walruses conferred among themselves. Things weren't going well at all, but no one wanted to break the news to the Old Man. He was the biggest and wisest walrus in the herd, and he knew his business and they didn't want to disappoint him or put him in a foul mood.

"What will we tell him?" whispered Basil, the walrus XO (Executive Officer). He well remembered how the Old Man had raved at him the last time the herd caught less than its quota of herring, and he had no desire for that experience again. Nevertheless, for several weeks the water level in the nearby bay had been falling constantly, and it had become necessary to travel farther to catch the dwindling supply of herring. Someone should tell the Old Man. But who? And how?

Finally, Basil spoke up: "Things are going pretty well, Boss," he said. The thought of the receding water line made his heart grow heavy, but he went on: "As a matter of fact, the beach seems to be getting larger."

The Old Man grunted. "Fine, fine," he said. "That will give us a bit more elbow room." He closed his eyes and continued basking in the sun.

The next day brought more trouble. A new herd of walruses moved in down the beach, and with the shortage of herring, the invasion could be dangerous. No one wanted to tell the Boss, though only he could take the steps necessary to meet the new competition. Basil approached the Old Man. After some small talk, he said, "Oh, by the way, Boss, a new herd seems to have moved into our territory." The Old Man's eyes snapped open, and he filled his great lungs in preparation for a mighty bellow. But Basil added quickly, "Of course, we don't expect any trouble. They don't look like herring-eaters to me. More likely interested in minnows. And as you know, we don't bother with minnows ourselves."

The Old Man let out the air with a long sigh. "Good, good," he said. "No point in our getting excited over nothing then, is there?"

Things didn't get any better in the weeks that followed. One day, peering down from his rock, the Old Man noticed that part of the herd seemed to be missing. Summoning the XO, he grunted peevishly, "What's going on, Basil? Where is everyone?" Poor Basil didn't have the courage to tell the Old Man that many of the younger walruses were leaving to join the new herd. Clearing his throat nervously he said, "Well, Boss, we've been tightening up things a bit. You know, getting rid of some of the dead wood. After all, a herd is only as good as the walruses in it."

"Run a tight ship, I always say," the Old Man grunted. "Glad to hear that all is going so well."

Before long, everyone but Basil had left to join the new herd, and Basil realized that the time had come to tell the Old Man the facts. Terrified but determined, he flopped up to the large rock. "Chief," he said, "I have bad news. The rest of the herd has left you." The Old Walrus was so astonished that he couldn't even work up a good bellow. "Left me?" he cried. "All of them? But why? How could this happen?"

Basil didn't have the heart to tell him, so he merely shrugged helplessly.

"I can't understand it," the old Walrus said. "And just when everything was going so well."[7]

According to Ritchie, the moral of the story is: "What the Boss likes to hear isn't always what he needs to know." We would add, "How *can* he know if he hasn't created a *culture* of open conversation that facilitates effective communication, engages the talent and top performance of everyone toward shared goals, and clears the path for the accomplishment of those goals?

When you think about it, what really is culture? Today, "culture" is one of the most common words we use when talking about organizations. When a company is successful, we often refer to its "powerful culture." When organizations struggle, we sometimes say, "They have such a restrictive culture, they can't retain good people."

We suggest that culture is the environment created by the collective habitual behaviors of the people in the organization. Simply put, it's their habits.

These habits are things you can observe. Do people start and stop meetings on time, or are they typically late? Do they come prepared to meetings, or rush in at the last minute unprepared? Do they treat due dates as personal commitments, or as vague targets that are often missed? Are they open to feedback, or resentful when people try to make suggestions? Are they free with information, or do they hold it close to the chest? These are all habitual behaviors you can observe, and they create the culture of the organization.

The nature and frequency of leadership conversations in any organization are a huge part of its culture. Again, they are something you can observe. In fact, if you have eyes to see and ears to hear, you can observe not only the actions, but also the attitudes of people as they interact with one another. And you can observe the difference it makes when actions and attitudes are aligned with principles of effectiveness—when they unleash voice and performance instead of squelching it, and when they clear the path for top performance.

The good news is that through the 3 Leadership Conversations we talk about in this book, you can teach and nurture the foundational principles that create a culture of top performance. You can also teach the behaviors that grow out of these principles. In teaching these things, you can literally help change the culture of your organization. Once a critical mass[8] of the people in an organization makes Leadership Conversations habitual, a culture of "release" is created.

Think about the factors impacted by this kind of transformation—things such as structure, systems, rewards, decision making, and strategy. Without taking an extensive side trip into organizational theory, consider the potential of the leadership conversations to affect these factors. As the conversations become part of the culture, systems are constantly upgraded and improved due to the flow of feedback. Operational systems essentially become self-regulating. Strategies are refined and integrated as part of the normal operating process. Reward systems become more integrated and relevant. And the list goes on.

> What I think is being recognized more and more by savvy organizations is that it's not just the employees that are valuable to an organization, it's the relationships that they foster and manage that are critically important. It's those relationships that are the essence of your productive capacity.
>
> —MIKE COOK

Keep in mind that at the very core of a healthy organization is the synaptic interaction of those people who *are* the organization. The 3 Leadership Conversations facilitate that synaptic interaction. They are simple, practical, and implementable; but collectively, they are both the goal of a high-performance organization and the way in which that goal is achieved.

Like the wise farmer, the wise leader learns that if you prepare the soil, plant, nurture, and cultivate, over time you will reap what you sow. Although individual events like a storm or a drought can't always be predicted, the pattern can be predicted. If you seek to apply valid principles, you will, over time, create the culture that will unleash capacity and cultivate success.

Final Words

If you seek to live by the principles of contribution, trust, synergy, and empathy, you go a long way toward unleashing talent.

People who have a meaningful contribution to make are hard to stop. Once they know what that contribution is, they're already unleashed—at least in their minds and hearts. The Voice Conversation is a leader's vehicle to discover and crystallize that contribution.

People who feel trusted are confident. They know you have faith in them, that you rely on them to deliver, and this is a mighty motivator. Good people don't like to let others down, and a clear Win-Win Performance Agreement makes it far easier to deliver on commitments with precision. The resulting sense of accomplishment makes them feel more trustworthy, and trustworthiness leads to trust—the one thing that changes everything.

People who know how to Synergize are precious assets. They're not the envious credit hogs who get jealous when anyone else succeeds. They don't get defensive when someone disagrees with them; instead, they're delighted because the ensuing discussion leads to better alternatives. And they're unstoppable because they find new ways to clear the inevitable hurdles on the path to success.

People who are listened to with empathy discover more about themselves, their talents, and their passions. They feel freer to express their thoughts and ideas—freer to take risks, innovate, collaborate, learn new skills, and try new things. Empathy is a gift, not only to the person who's listened to, but also to the leader, the team, and the organization.

Collectively, unleashed people interacting effectively create the high-performance organization.

This last set of discussion questions in this book is intended to help you build that kind of a high-performance team. These are searching questions that will hopefully help you gauge for yourself your readiness to lead an "unleashed" team.

DISCUSSION QUESTIONS

1. Do you really want to unleash the talent of your people? Are you ready to go down that path?
2. Are you the kind of person who can let go of control and release the team to create its own path to success?
3. As a leader, can you find it in yourself to spend a good deal of time in conversation—not only in formal conversations, but in huddles and one-on-ones with team members—or would you rather leave them alone to do their jobs?
4. Do you really believe in the value of principles such as contribution, trust, and synergy? If so, how do you think you can you leverage those principles to unleash the talent in your team?
5. Are you the sort of leader who prefers to oversee and supervise, or to "run ahead and alongside" your team on their path to success?
6. Are you able to invest the personal energy it will take to make a strong human connection with each member of your team?
7. As you read the Epilogue to this book, ask yourself this question: "As a leader who wants my team to succeed, where should I focus my best effort and energy?"

EYES TO SEE

Everyone has inside of him a piece of good news. The good
news is that you don't know how great you can be! How
much you can love! What you can accomplish! And what
your potential is!

—ANNE FRANK, *The Diary of a Young Girl*

AUTHOR NOTE Some years ago, while I was leading a medium-size organization with six divisions, I found that one of those divisions was going to need a new manager. As I tried to determine who should be offered that position, John's name came to mind.

I was surprised I'd even thought of him. While he was very effective operationally, he was known to be somewhat blunt in his communication with others. This division had a lot of relationship issues, and I had naturally assumed that in addition to the requisite knowledge and skills, the next manager would need to have a strong, outgoing personality to create unity and interpersonal healing.

Because I'd had some previous interactions with John (which I would now call Voice Conversations), I knew that deep inside, he really had a very tender heart, but it didn't come across very often. Nevertheless, for some reason I kept having the feeling that he had the very talents this group needed.

When I submitted John's name as division manager, there were a lot of raised eyebrows. However, based on my recommendation, he was eventually offered the position. He and I sat down together and talked about the issues and the desired results, and I did everything I could to help facilitate his success.

What I soon discovered was that every time John and I would have a conversation about a problem in the division, he would immediately target the real issue and go the extra mile to help and support the people involved. I found that John was able to reach out not only to those who were the superstars, but also to those were on the fringes. He would quietly work with them, strengthening them and helping them develop the skills they needed to be successful.

Under John's leadership, it wasn't long before people began to flourish, issues got resolved, and engagement increased. Soon people began to recognize John's efforts, and his example became a spark that inspired everyone in the division to improve and to be more understanding of and helpful to others. Though some of his conversations were still a bit blunt at times, people began to see what was in his heart, and he ended up being very successful and respected as the division manager. Where I had worried about his ability to work with people, that turned out to be his greatest strength as others began to realize how much he really cared.

My experience with John taught me a lot. It taught me to not be too quick to judge people, but to try to be open to what is deep within them and give them opportunities to let their strengths blossom.

It taught me that we don't necessarily need to pass over people because they have a few rough edges or think we have to completely change their personality if they're going to be useful. If we have eyes to see the gold hidden beneath those rough edges, we can encourage them to give voice to their inner best and create the environment in which their strengths can flourish.

It taught me the importance of having Voice Conversations. If I'd never had those initial conversations with John, I would never have been aware of his caring personality or his potential strength. Those he would have been able to influence in positive ways would have missed the growth his efforts enabled, and our division would have missed out on much of the significant growth we achieved as a result.

It also taught me that I needed to develop "eyes to see" what was right in front of me. It made me wonder what other "diamonds in the rough" I needed to get to know.

As we mentioned in the Prologue to this book—just like t
who blindly passed by world-class violinist Joshua Be
that cold January morning in the Washington, D.C., Me
as leaders and coaches, we often don't even see the talen
potential of those with whom we work.

Yet, unleashing that talent and potential is the key to
ating high-performance teams and organizations.

Often, too, we don't clearly "see" our own roles as lea
coaches and mentors. To be in any leadership role is b
wonderful opportunity and a serious responsibility. Wh
that role is formal or informal—as president of a global
nization of thousands, or manager of a team of three
parent—we are in a position to influence others and worl
them to accomplish marvelous things.

As we said in Chapter 1, the single factor that makes
found positive difference in the performance of indivi
and companies worldwide is *leaders who unleash the tal*
those with whom they work.

Some of us are in positions that more naturally le
to find joy in unleashing the talents and abilities of o
If we're parents, we're generally thrilled when we se
children grow, develop, and succeed. If we work in ph
therapy, we feel great satisfaction when we're able to
people overcome the ill effects of an accident or illness
coach an athletic team, we celebrate when our team dev
the skill to earn a victory. If we teach children or adul
feel happy when our students gain new knowledge or sk
each instance, we *see* our own success in terms of facili
the success of others.

On the other hand, some of us are in positions that
easily lead us to focus on finding satisfaction in other t
such as increased personal income, recognition, accolac
promotion. This is especially true when we're in more v

leadership roles in for-profit organizations that are not directly connected with work that is human development or humanitarian in nature. In these situations, it's sometimes harder to see our leadership roles in terms of genuinely caring about and unleashing the talents of others. Nevertheless, we again assert that this is where real joy, satisfaction and, ultimately, success come in any leadership role.

So how do we develop eyes to see?

It's often been said that *seeing* is *believing*. But the opposite is also true. If you *believe* there truly are principles of effectiveness—and you *believe* that, despite the challenges, living in harmony with those principles and helping others to do so will create the best possible outcomes in your life and in your leadership—then you will *see* people and opportunities differently. You won't see people as objects to be used or machines to be fixed or tossed; you'll see them as developing, growing beings of talent, intelligence, depth, and great potential—beings whose contributions can help better the world. You won't see your role as one of dictating or controlling; you'll see it as one of unleashing the talent and passion to contribute that lie within those you've been trusted to lead.

Based on how you *see* others and yourself, then, you will *do* the things you think will enable you to fulfill your role in that way, and you will *get* the positive results that are based on principle-centered beliefs.

One of those things you'll do is to have frequent, meaningful *conversations* with those you lead that will free them to contribute in the best possible way. Remember, you can never *not* communicate. You're communicating all the time, and those communications—both verbal and nonverbal—are either helping release voice and performance and clearing the path, or they're not.

If they are, you're doing the things "leaders" do. If they're not, you may be doing things a manager or an individual contributor might do, but you're not doing what leaders do. And what kind of culture is created as a result?

As you consider this material, keep this in mind: If you want to improve your leadership, but your past experience—or lack of experience—has not brought you to the point of belief and vision in the reality and power of these principles, remember that just *desiring* to believe will start you on the path. Motivated by that desire, just jump in and try the 3 Leadership Conversations. The guides make it simple. Study the chapters on each of the conversations and learn more deeply as you go.

Also keep in mind that as you engage in these leadership conversations, more and more you will recognize that you're not only helping others, you're developing new talents and abilities yourself. You're becoming a better listener. You're paying more attention to people. You're becoming more aware of their talents and how they can better contribute to your team or organization. You're changing your paradigm of an effective leader. You're becoming a teacher, a coach, and a genuine source of help to those you lead. You're significantly improving the quantity, quality, and nature of the contribution of your team to the organization as a whole. You're helping create a culture that unleashes talent and facilitates top performance.

You're going to make mistakes. You likely won't do things perfectly, particularly at first. But let's be real—none of us is really "perfect" in anything we do. However, to the degree we really believe in the principles of effectiveness and apply them in our lives and in our leadership, we become better in doing and in getting the results we want to achieve.

We end with the promise we made to you in the Prologue:

If you will engage with us by reading this book and begin to hold genuine leadership conversations with those around you using the Conversation Guides throughout the book, you will:

- ▶ Develop a new leadership mindset and skillset which will significantly strengthen your relationships with those you lead.
- ▶ Develop confidence in your ability to recognize and unleash the talents of others.
- ▶ Develop a growing awareness that as you unleash the talents of others, you are unleashing your own as well.

As you've read this book, we hope you've tried holding some leadership conversations. If you have, are some of these things beginning to happen for you? We genuinely hope you have, because we know it will make an enormous difference in your leadership and in your life.

If you've not tried them yet, we encourage you to do so, for unleashing talent to contribute—in others as well as in yourself—is truly one of life's greatest joys.

APPENDIX A

3 Leadership Conversations
Transparent Agenda

VOICE

"This voice also encompasses the soul of organizations that will survive, thrive, and profoundly impact the future of the world.

Voice is *unique personal significance*—significance that is revealed as we face our greatest challenges and which makes us equal to them.

Voice lies at the nexus of *talent* (your natural gifts and strengths), *passion* (those things that naturally energize, excite, motivate, and inspire you), *need* (including what the world needs enough to pay you for), and *conscience* (that still, small voice within that assures you of what is right and that prompts you to actually do it). When you engage in work that taps your talent and fuels your passion—that rises out of a great need in the world that you feel drawn by conscience to meet—therein lies your voice, your calling, your soul's code."

STEPHEN R. COVEY, *THE 8TH HABIT*

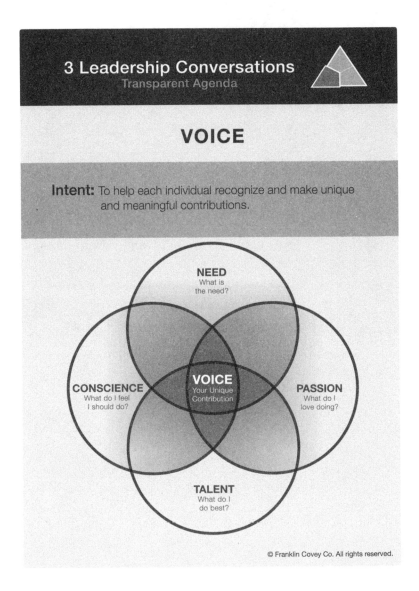

3 Leadership Conversations
Transparent Agenda

VOICE

Intent: To help each individual recognize and make unique and meaningful contributions.

NEED
What is
the need?

CONSCIENCE
What do I feel
I should do?

VOICE
Your Unique
Contribution

PASSION
What do I
love doing?

TALENT
What do I
do best?

3 Leadership Conversations
Transparent Agenda

VOICE

How to Use: Ask each question and then add your perspective—or use your answers to the questions to generate a conversation with the other person.

1. NEED (external or internal)

    a. What unmet needs and opportunities do you see among our customers, within our business, or in the marketplace?

    b. What is the ONE thing you could do to make the greatest contribution?

2. PASSION

    a. What have you always loved doing?

    b. What job or career-related opportunities are you most excited about?

3. TALENT

    a. What are your interests, talents, and capabilities and how could you develop them further?

    b. What could you do well that you're not currently doing?

4. CONSCIENCE

    a. What values or principles are most important to you?

    b. What part of your work do you feel best about, and what would make it more meaningful?

3 Leadership Conversations
Transparent Agenda

VOICE CONVERSATION WATCHOUTS

Attitudes to Avoid

- "This 'voice' stuff is irrelevant; *my* job is to make sure people do *their* job."
- "We talk about people's potential in their annual performance review."
- "I'll do this if I have time."
- "Who cares if people are *fired up* as long as they're doing the job they were hired to do?"
- "I assume people will naturally trust me enough to share what's important to them."
- "I already know what's important to others."
- "As long as we're making money, what does it matter?"

3 Leadership Conversations
Transparent Agenda

PERFORMANCE

In a well-conducted performance conversation, the individual worker agrees on **what** is important, **why** it is important, **how** it is to be accomplished, and how it can be **tracked and improved**. The worker begins to both see and share commitment to the overall organizational vision, mission, strategies, and goals. It is not a one-way conversation, particularly when the worker is not new on the job. It is a win-win-win conversation—a win for the organization, a win for the boss, and a win for the worker in helping them align and achieve their most important goals and objectives.

TALENT UNLEASHED

"As a rule there are in everyone all sorts of good ideas, ready like tinder. But much of this tinder catches fire...only when it meets some flame or spark...from some other person."

-ALBERT SCHWEITZER

APPENDIX A

3 Leadership Conversations
Transparent Agenda

1–DESIRED RESULTS

How to Use: Discuss and come to an agreement on each factor listed below.

What needs to be done?

1. What are the team's top two or three goals?

2. How will we measure success?

3. What are your top two or three individual goals—the goals you need to achieve in order to make your contribution?

4. How do your individual goals connect to the team's top goals? Why are your goals important?

5. Are your goals realistic and achievable?

6. How have you translated these goals into plans (i.e., who will do what by when)?

7. How will you measure your success?

Watchouts

- Avoid taking on too many goals.

- Don't be one-sided or dictatorial. Listen with the intent to understand.

3 Leadership Conversations
Transparent Agenda

2—GUIDELINES

How to Use: Discuss and come to an agreement on each factor listed below.

What standards need to be met?

1. What other people need to be involved in this conversation, and what are their expectations?

2. How will your work impact other teams or functions?

3. What policies and/or procedures are in place?

4. Are there any related ecological, quality, safety, or legal requirements to consider?

5. Are there any political or cultural dynamics to consider?

Watchouts

- Don't create unnecessary policies.
- Don't ignore essential policies.

3 Leadership Conversations
Transparent Agenda

3—RESOURCES

How to Use: Discuss and come to an agreement on each factor listed below.

Who/what is needed to accomplish the desired results?

1. What people and other resources (e.g., information, financial, training, etc.) are needed and available?

2. Who can authorize access to the necessary resources?

3. What potential barriers need to be resolved?

4. Is there "game-changing" information or technology that could be utilized?

5. Are there any people or resources that could be repurposed?

Watchouts

- Don't give up too quickly. Is there a different way to obtain the necessary resources?

3 Leadership Conversations
Transparent Agenda

4 – ACCOUNTABILITY

How to Use: Discuss and come to an agreement on each factor listed below.

How will we track performance?

1. What are the measurable, influenceable, and predictive activities (lead indicators)?

2. Who will receive information and how will tracking take place?

3. What key milestones will be achieved along the way?

4. How often will we meet to review progress?

5. If necessary, how will we modify our agreement?

Watchouts

- Don't forget that accountability is a two-way, agreement-based process. It is something you *share*, not something you *do* to someone.

- Don't assume that frequent accountability will take place without a systematized communication and review process.

- Don't use accountability as a threat. Instead, use it as a process for creating meaning and engagement.

3 Leadership Conversations
Transparent Agenda

5—CONSEQUENCES

How to Use: Discuss and come to an agreement on each factor listed below.

1. When goals are achieved, what are the implications:
   - For the customer (internal/external)?
   - For the organization?
   - For the team?
   - For the individual?
   - For other stakeholders?

2. If goals are not achieved, what are the implications:
   - For the customer (internal/external)?
   - For the organization?
   - For the team?
   - For the individual?
   - For other stakeholders?

3. Are modifications to the agreement needed?

Watchouts

   - Avoid creating unintended expectations.

3 Leadership Conversations
Transparent Agenda

PERFORMANCE CONVERSATION WATCHOUTS

Avoid

- Assuming people know where to focus.
- Listening to reply rather than to understand.
- Failing to differentiate between the *many important tasks* and the *vital few.*
- Failing to make specific links to overall organizational objectives.
- Giving superficial attention to issues, questions, and challenges.
- Pushing your agenda rather than seeking mutual agreement.

3 Leadership Conversations
Transparent Agenda

CLEAR-THE-PATH

Leaders can be a source of help to those they lead. They can look ahead and try to discern what may be needed. They can watch and learn from what the team is doing and see what team members need to keep going and/or improve. They can then teach or pass on what they learn. They can coach. They can help prevent problems and anticipate opportunities. Each team member can work within his or her Circle of Influence to help and support others. This is how quantum performance improvement comes.

TALENT UNLEASHED

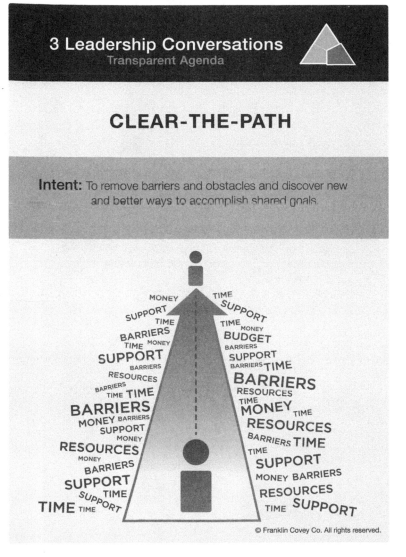

3 Leadership Conversations
Transparent Agenda

CLEAR-THE-PATH

Intent: To remove barriers and obstacles and discover new and better ways to accomplish shared goals.

3 Leadership Conversations
Transparent Agenda

CLEAR-THE-PATH

How to Use: Ask each question—or use your answers to the questions to generate a discussion or make a request.

Questions:

1. What are you working on and how is it going?

2. What are you learning?

3. What obstacles are getting in your way?

4. If you could change one thing to improve your progress, what would it be?

5. What can team members do to remove barriers for each other?

6. What new opportunities are you seeing?

7. How can I best help you?

CLEAR-THE-PATH CONVERSATION WATCHOUTS

Attitudes to Avoid

- "If people need me, they know where to find me."

- "I'm already working long hours just to stay on top of what others are supposed to be doing."

- "I've got all the answers."

3 Leadership Conversations
Transparent Agenda

FOUR GOVERNING PRINCIPLES

Principle 1: Contribution

- Make a positive difference.
- Add value.

OPPOSITE: Greed, apathy, selfishness

Principle 2: Trust

- Be trustworthy.
- Make and keep commitments.

OPPOSITE: Distrust, suspicion, cynicism

Principle 3: Synergy

- Merge differences in unity of purpose to create a power greater than the sum of the parts.

OPPOSITE: Scarcity

Principle 4: Empathy

- Listen to genuinely understand.

OPPOSITE: Listen with intent to judge, criticize, editoralize, prepare a response, or share your own autobiography.

3 Leadership Conversations
Transparent Agenda

Reminders

- You are having conversations all the time—intentional or unintentional, formal, or informal. Make sure you are communicating what you want to communicate.

- Everyone has potential for extraordinary contribution. Make sure you "see" the people you work with as expanding, growing contributors with unique and extraordinary contributions to make.

Opportunities

- You observe a team member who does not seem enthused about work or who doubts his or her ability. This is your chance to have a meaningful "Voice Conversation."

- You observe an individual or team that seems to be working hard but not really achieving meaningful results. This is your chance to have a quality "Performance Conversation."

- You see your team working hard, but you want to facilitate greater results. This is you opportunity to have a helpful "Clear-the-Path Conversation."

APPENDIX B

Agreement Between _____   **Date** _____

Contribution Statement:

Desired Results
What are the results you are trying to achieve?
_____
_____
_____
_____

Guidelines
What key criteria, standards, policies, or procedures should be followed?
_____
_____
_____
_____

Resources
What people, budget, and tools are available?
_____
_____
_____
_____

Accountability
How will we give feedback? How often?
_____
_____
_____
_____

Consequences
What are the rewards if the agreement is fulfilled?
_____
_____
_____

What are the consequences if the agreement is not fulfilled?
_____
_____
_____
_____

TALENT UNLEASHED

WIN-WIN PERFORMANCE AGREEMENT

Agreement Between VP of Sales and Jackie   **Date** September 1

Contribution Statement

I will bring my deep project-management expertise and people-leadership skills to help my department and our company achieve our sales goals.

Desired Results
What are the results you are trying to achieve?

- To be an effective project leader with full ownership for training of account executives on a new "go to market" approach of our product.
- To meet quarterly and meet annual sales goals with new products.
- To engage in new and challenging opportunities that provide ongoing learning and development experiences.

Guidelines
What key criteria, standards, policies, or procedures should be followed?

- Weekly communication with Sales and Marketing leaders are to be attended in person.
- Training on the new product must be done while the current product continues to be successfully marketed and sold.

Resources
What people, budget, and tools are available?

- Administrative assistance from the sales leader's current support staff.
- Predetermined budgets for training and ongoing coaching meetings.
- 10 to 15 hours a week of assistance from existing members of the training team.

Accountability
How will we give feedback? How often?

- Weekly update meetings will be held each Monday where progress will be shared.
- The Product Rollout Scoreboard will be updated daily with current information.
- A monthly meeting with the sales leader will be held to review the overall progress and make any needed adjustments.

Consequences
What are the rewards if the agreement is fulfilled?

- The company hits and exceeds revenue targets for new product.
- I gain additional experience with new opportunities using the previously "untapped" talent.
- I receive bonus pay tied to the success of revenue targets.

What are the consequences if the agreement is not fulfilled?

- Both the company and I fail to receive the positive consequences listed above.

ENDNOTES

Prologue

1. www.pewresearch.org/fact-tank/2015/05/11/millennials-surpass-gen-xers-as-the-largest-generation-in-u-s-labor-force/
2. www.gallup.com/businessjournal/191459/millennials-job-hopping-generation.aspx?g_source=WORKPLACE&g_medium=topic&g_campaign=tiles

Chapter 1

1. Bill Conaty, Ram Charan, *The Talent Masters*, Cornerstone Digital, 2011. www.amazon.com/Talent-Masters-Leaders-People-Numbers/dp/1847940722/ref=sr_1_2?ie=UTF8&qid=1453755189&sr=8- 2&keywords=ram+charan+talent+masters
2. *The Teachings of Ptahhotep: The Oldest Book in the World* (Kindle Locations 181–185). African Tree Press. Kindle Edition.
3. Robert J. Anderson and William A. Adams, *Mastering Leadership: An Integrated Framework for Breakthrough Performance and Extraordinary Business Results*, John Wiley & Sons, 2015, 22.
4. Ibid
5. www.gallup.com/businessjournal/182321/employees-lot-managers.aspx
6. Edward M. Hallowell, *Shine: Using Brain Science to Get the Best from Your People*, Harvard Business Press, 2013, n.p. books.google.com/books?id=hfnQlqg42rIC&dq=The+all-powerful+propeller
7. henryfordleadershipandlegacy.weebly.com/early-life.html
8. See for example "Measuring the Strategic Readiness of Intangible Assets," *Harvard Business Review*, Feb. 1, 2004.
9. "Annual Study of Intangible Asset Market Value," Ocean Tomo, LLC. March 4, 2015. www.oceantomo.com/2015/03/04/2015-intangible-asset-market-value-study/
10. en.wikiquote.org/wiki/N._R._Narayana_Murthy
11. Allan Freed and Dave Ulrich, "Calculating the Market Value of Leadership," *Harvard Business Review*, Apr. 3 2015. hbr.org/2015/04/calculating-the-market-value-of-leadership

Chapter 2

1. Sydney Finkelstein, "What Amazing Bosses Do Differently," *Harvard Business Review*, Nov. 29, 2015. hbr.org/2015/11/what-amazing-bosses-do-differently

2. Stephen R. Covey, *The 8th Habit: From Effectiveness to Greatness*, 97.
3. www2.deloitte.com/content/dam/Deloitte/global/Documents/ About-Deloitte/gx-millenial-survey- 2016-exec-summary.pdf
4. www.gallup.com/businessjournal/182321/employees-lot-managers.aspx
5. See Dave Ulrich, *The Leadership Capital Index*, Berrett-Koehler Publishers, 2015, 9.
6. Stephen R. Covey, *The 8th Habit: From Effectiveness to Greatness*, 5.
7. Steve Jobs, Stanford University Commencement Address, 2005.
8. "For Tunisian Entrepreneur, Another Person's Trash Is Her Business," Knowledge@Wharton, June 25, 2013. knowledge.wharton.upenn.edu/ article/for-tunisian-entrepreneur-another-persons-trash-is-her-business/
9. Ibid
10. Malcolm Gladwell, *Outliers: The Story of Success*, Little, Brown and Co., 2008, 37–38.
11. Gladwell, 104.
12. Chris DeRose, "How Google Uses Data to Create a Better Worker," *Atlantic*, Oct. 7, 2013. www.theatlantic.com/business/archive/2013/10/ how-google-uses-data-to-build-a-better-worker/280347/
13. James M. Kouzes and Barry Z. Posner, *Credibility: How Leaders Gain and Lose It, Why People Demand It*, Jossey-Bass, 2011, 135.
14. Ty Kiisel, "82 Percent of People Don't Trust the Boss to Tell the Truth," *Forbes*, Jan. 30, 2013. www.forbes.com/sites/tykiisel/2013/01/30/82-percent-of-people-dont-trust-the-boss-to-tell-the- truth/
15. Blaine Lee, *The Power Principle: Influence With Honor*, Free Press, 1998, 105.

Chapter 3

1. Howard M. Guttman, *Great Business Teams: Cracking the Code for Standout Performance*, Guttman Development Strategies, Wiley, 2008.
2. Peter Senge, *The Fifth Discipline*, 1995, 13.
3. Susan Sorenson, "How Employee Engagement Drives Growth," *Gallup Business Journal,* June 20, 2013. www.gallup.com/businessjournal/ 163130/employee-engagement-drives-growth.aspx
4. Ray Williams, "Why Performance Reviews Won't Improve Performance," *Psychology Today,* Nov. 7, 2012. www.psychologytoday.com/blog/ wired-success/201211why-performance-reviews-dont-improve-performance
5. B. Hoffman, et al., "Rater Source Effects Are Alive and Well After All," *Personnel Psychology*, 63 (2010), 119–151. 6 Jena McGregor, "Study Finds That Basically Every Single Person Hates Performance Reviews," *The Washington Post,* Jan. 27, 2014. www.washingtonpost.com/news/

on-leadership/wp/2014/01/27/study-finds-that- basically-every-single-person-hates-performance-reviews/

7. Cited in Vauhini Vara, "The Push Against Performance Reviews," *The New Yorker*, Jul. 24, 2015. www.newyorker.com/business/currency/ the-push-against-performance-reviews

8. Samuel A. Culbert, "Yes, Everyone Really Does Hate Performance Reviews," *The Wall Street Journal*, Apr. 11, 2010. www.wsj.com/articles/ SB127093422486175363

9. Samuel A. Culbert, "Performance Reviews Are Corporate America's Curse on Itself," *Los Angeles Times*, Feb. 12, 2015. http://www.latimes.com/ opinion/op-ed/la-oe-0213-culbert-performance-reviews-20150213-story. html

10. hbr.org/2011/05/the-power-of-small-wins

11. Frédéric Laloux, *Reinventing Organizations*, Nelson Parker, 2014, 242.

12. Jack Welch with Suzy Welch, *Winning*, pp. 3, 4.

13. Melissa Dahl, "It's Time to Kill the Performance Review," *New York* magazine, Jun. 1, 2015. nymag.com/scienceofus/2015/05/time-to-revamp-the-performance-review.html

Chapter 4

1. John F. Kennedy, "Excerpt from the special message to the Congress on urgent national needs," May 25, 1961. www.nasa.gov/vision/space/ features/jfk_speech_text.html#.VqAvpfkrLDc

2. Jim Collins, *How the Mighty Fall*, Harper-Collins, 2009, 56.

3. Harry Chambers, *My Way of the Highway*, Berrett-Koehler Publishers, 2004.

4. L. David Marquet, *Turn the Ship Around!* Penguin, 2012, 80–82.

5. Aaron De Smet, et al., "Unlocking the Potential of Frontline Managers," *Insights & Publications*, McKinsey & Company, August 2009, italics added. www.mckinsey.com/insights/organization/unlocking_the_ potential_of_frontline_managers

Chapter 5

1. www.lectlaw.com/files/fun28.htm

2. Adam Smith, *The Theory of Moral Sentiments*, 2nd ed., London: A. Millar, 1761, 214.

3. Edmund L. Andrews, "Greenspan Concedes Error on Regulation," *The New York Times*, Oct. 23, 2008. www.nytimes.com/2008/10/24/ business/economy/24panel.html?_r=2&hp&oref=slog

4. Fred Reichheld, *The Ultimate Question*, Harvard Business School Press, 2006, 4.

5. Francis Fukuyama, *Trust: The Social Virtues and the Creation of Prosperity*, Free Press, 1996, 28.
6. See Sean Covey, *The 7 Habits of Highly Effective College Students*, FranklinCovey, 2014.
7. J. Bonner Ritchie, *American Management Review*, 1970s.
8. For more information on how to effectively listen with empathy, refer to *The 7 Habits of Highly Effective People*, Habit 5: "Seek First to Understand, Then to Be Understood."

In social dynamics, "critical mass" is a sufficient number of adopters of an innovation in a social system so that the rate of adoption becomes self-sustaining and creates further growth. There are various theories about how to quantify critical mass in an organization, such as "the one-third hypothesis," "tipping point," "viral phenomenon," and "the bandwagon effect." The key point is that in any organization of more than a few people, there is some number less than everybody that will create a critical mass and the "culture" of the organization will change.

ABOUT THE AUTHORS

Bios on Shawn D. Moon, Todd Davis,
Michael Simpson, and A. Roger Merrill
are on the pages that follow.

SHAWN D. MOON

*Executive Vice President, Strategic Markets,
FranklinCovey*

Shawn Moon is a co-author of *Talent Unleashed: 3 Leadership
Conversations to Ignite the Unlimited Potential in People*, Franklin-
Covey's newest book of powerful leadership insights and practices.
This book highlights liberating concepts, conversations, and principles built to inspire leaders and their teams to create a culture that
is rich in trust, clarity, and empowerment. The author shares knowledge gained from working with thousands of corporate leaders in
industries spanning the global workforce.

Moon has nearly 30 years experience in leadership and management, sales and marketing, program development, and consulting
services. His deep knowledge and robust experience inspires others
to become leaders through personal effectiveness and execution.

In his role as Executive Vice President at FranklinCovey, Moon
is responsible for the company's U.S. and international direct offices,
the Sales Performance Practice, and the Execution and Speed of
Trust Practices. Additionally, he oversees FranklinCovey's Government Business, Facilitator Initiatives, and Public Programs.

Moon was previously a Principal with Mellon Financial Corpo-
ration where he was responsible for business development for their
Human Resources outsourcing services. He coordinated activities
within the consulting and advisory community for Mellon Human
Resources and Investor Solutions. Prior to November 2002, Moon
served as the company's Vice-President of Business Development
for its Training Process Outsourcing Group, managing vertical
market sales for nine of the company's business units, and managed
the eastern regional sales office.

Moon is the author of *The Ultimate Competitive Advantage:
Why Your People Make All the Difference* and *6 Practices You Need
to Engage Them*, as well as several white papers and monographs

that outline essential tactics for building a winning culture. Shawn is a member of the Association for Talent Development (ATD) and sits on the boards of Zerorez® and the Utah Regional Ballet.

TODD DAVIS

Chief People Officer and Executive Vice President, FranklinCovey

Todd Davis is a co-author of *Talent Unleashed: 3 Leadership Conversations to Ignite the Unlimited Potential in People*, FranklinCovey's newest book of powerful leadership insights and practices. The book highlights liberating concepts, conversations, and principles built to inspire leaders and their teams to create a culture that is rich in trust, clarity, and empowerment. The author shares knowledge gained from working with thousands of corporate leaders in industries that span the global workforce.

Over the past 30 years, Davis has practiced and refined his skills and knowledge of human resources, talent development, executive recruiting, sales, and marketing. With FranklinCovey for more than 20 years, he currently serves as Executive Vice President and Chief People Officer. As a member of FranklinCovey's executive team, Davis is responsible for global talent development, which includes more than 40 offices in 160 countries.

Prior to this role, Davis was a Director for FranklinCovey's Innovations Group. In this vital role, he led the development of content in many of FranklinCovey's core offerings. Davis contributes to the development of new offerings, containing the company's world renowned content.

Davis also served as FranklinCovey's Director of Recruitment for several years, where he led a team responsible for attracting, hiring, and retaining top talent for the organization, which included more than 3,500 employees.

For more than 25 years, Davis has been entertaining and inspiring people throughout the world with his deep understanding of leadership, employee engagement, and talent management. He has delivered numerous keynote addresses and speeches at top industry conferences and associations, at annual corporate events, and for FranklinCovey clients, many of which are Fortune 100 and 500 companies. His topics include leadership, personal and interpersonal effectiveness, employee engagement, talent management, culture, and change management.

Prior to FranklinCovey, Davis worked in the medical industry for a decade, recruiting physicians and medical executives, as well as marketing physician services to hospitals and clients throughout the U.S.

Davis served on the Board of Directors for HR.com and is a member of the Association for Talent Development (ATD) and the Society for Human Resource Management.

MICHAEL SIMPSON

Global Managing Director for Executive Coaching, FranklinCovey

Michael Simpson is co-author of *Talent Unleashed: 3 Leadership Conversations to Ignite the Unlimited Potential in People,* Franklin-Covey's newest book of powerful leadership insights and practices. This book highlights liberating concepts, conversations, and principles built to inspire leaders and their teams to create a culture that is rich in trust, clarity, and empowerment. The author shares knowledge gained from working with thousands of corporate leaders in industries spanning the global workforce.

For 30 years, Simpson has been an internationally sought after executive coach, leadership consultant, and keynote speaker. His practical, business experience is in teaching, advising, and coaching many of the world's top business leaders and teams. He coached and consulted with leaders in over 35 countries in leadership development, strategic planning, goal execution, building high performance-based teams, and high trust organizational cultures.

For the past 21 years, Simpson has been a Global Delivery Senior Consultant in FranklinCovey's Strategy Execution, Leadership, and Trust Practices. He is co-founder and Global Managing Director for the FranklinCovey-Columbia University Executive Coaching Certification Program.

Simpson was formerly a Principal Consultant for the global management consulting firms Ernst & Young (EY) Change Management Practice in Washington, D.C. and PricewaterhouseCooper's (PwC) Strategic and Organizational Change Practice in New York, NY. He held executive leadership positions for two leading technology companies as Vice President of Sales and Marketing and Vice President of Business Development.

Simpson holds a master's in Organizational Behavior from Columbia University and a bachelor's from Brigham Young University's Kennedy School of International Relations. He holds a

Graduate Studies Certificate in Conflict Resolution and Mediation from Columbia's International Center for Cooperation and Conflict Resolution (ICCCR). He is a certified executive coach from Columbia's Executive Coaching Certification Program; a certified coach from Marshall Goldsmith's Stakeholder Executive Coaching program; a certified coach with Inside-out GROW coaching; and a certified coach from University of Maryland's The Art and Practice of Coaching Leaders.

Simpson has authored several leadership and coaching books and articles including: *Unlocking Potential: 7 Coaching Skills That Transform Individuals, Teams, and Organizations*; *Ready, Aim, Excel*; *Your Seeds of Greatness: 10,000 of the World's Greatest Leadership Quotes*; *The Execution-focused Leader*; and *Building Team and Organizational Trust* with Stephen M.R. Covey.

A. ROGER MERRILL

Executive Coach, Consultant, and Bestselling Author

Roger Merrill is a co-author of *Talent Unleashed: 3 Leadership Conversations to Ignite the Unlimited Potential in People,* Franklin-Covey's newest book of powerful leadership insights and practices. This book highlights liberating concepts, conversations, and principles built to inspire leaders and their teams to create a culture that is rich in trust, clarity, and empowerment. The author shares knowledge gained from working with thousands of corporate leaders in industries spanning the global workforce.

Merrill has more than 40 years of experience as a line manager, senior executive, executive coach, consultant, and teacher, and was one of the co-founders of Covey Leadership Center (now Franklin-Covey Co.). Merrill specializes in coaching senior leaders and helping organizations improve performance and develop leaders.

As an executive coach, speaker, consultant, and trainer, Merrill has worked with over 600 different organizations in more than 30 countries and addressed domestic and international audiences ranging to more than 20,000. He holds a degree in business management and has done extensive graduate work in organizational behavior and adult learning.

Merrill is co-author (with Stephen R. Covey and Rebecca R. Merrill) of the international best seller *First Things First.* He is the author of *Connections: Quadrant II Time Management,* co-author of *The Nature of Leadership,* and contributing author to *Principle-Centered Leadership.* His book *Life Matters: Creating a Dynamic Balance of Work, Family, Time, and Money* (co-authored with his wife, Rebecca) was recognized by Soundview Executive Summaries as one of the 30 best business books of 2004. As a writer and thought leader, his books have sold over 2.5 million copies and have been translated into more than a dozen languages.

"PEOPLE ARE OUR **MOST IMPORTANT** ASSET."

Every company pays lip service to this platitude, but **how many companies really embrace it**?

People can sustain — or ruin — your brand. If your people lack excitement, are indifferent, or even feel alienated from the company, your competitive advantage will disappear.

In *The Ultimate Competitive Advantage*, FranklinCovey thought leaders Shawn D. Moon and Sue Dathe-Douglass, lay out the steps leaders can take to tap into their organizations' most valuable and unique resource: **people.**

From the company that brought you *The 7 Habits of Highly Effective People*, *The Ultimate Competitive Advantage* offers six highly effective practices that will propel your organization to success by unleashing the potential of your people.

Each practice in *The Ultimate Competitive Advantage* is based on fundamental principles that hold true across all cultures, industries, organizations, and agencies, from the necessity of being proactive to the importance of building win-win, high trust relationships, to executing strategy effectively. Implementing these practices is the key to making a distinctive difference in the marketplace.

The Ultimate Competitive Advantage will **enable your organization to achieve remarkable results and become an industry standout** by leveraging your most important asset: your people.

AVAILABLE WHEREVER BOOKS ARE SOLD.

THE ULTIMATE COMPETITIVE ADVANTAGE

FranklinCovey is a global company specializing in organizational performance improvement. We help organizations achieve results that require a change in human behavior.

Our expertise is in seven areas:

LEADERSHIP

Develops highly effective leaders who engage others to achieve results.

EXECUTION

Enables organizations to execute strategies that require a change in human behavior.

PRODUCTIVITY

Equips people to make high-value choices and execute with excellence in the midst of competing priorities.

TRUST

Builds a high-trust culture of collaboration and engagement, resulting in greater speed and lower costs.

SALES PERFORMANCE

Transforms the buyer-seller relationship by helping clients succeed.

CUSTOMER LOYALTY

Drives faster growth and improves frontline performance with accurate customer- and employee-loyalty data.

EDUCATION

Helps schools transform their performance by unleashing the greatness in every educator and student.

ATTEND A **COMPLIMENTARY WEBCAST**

Join one of our experts for a complimentary, live webcast and learn more about the *3 Leadership Conversations to Ignite the Unlimited Potential in People.*

FranklinCovey offers live webcasts in a variety of areas related to Leadership, Execution, Productivity, Trust, Sales Performance, Customer Loyalty, and Education.

For more information, or to register, visit www.franklincovey.com/ webcast-series.

OUR MOST POPULAR WEBCASTS

These webcasts highlight key concepts, demonstrate participant tools and resources, and discuss implementation options. Some of our more popular webcasts are:

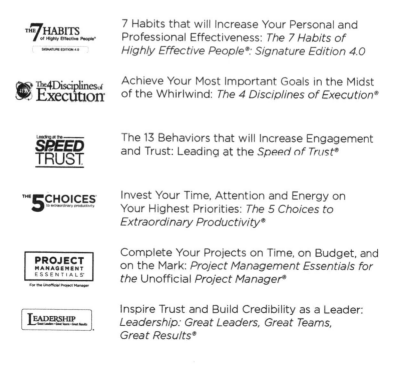

7 Habits that will Increase Your Personal and Professional Effectiveness: *The 7 Habits of Highly Effective People®: Signature Edition 4.0*

Achieve Your Most Important Goals in the Midst of the Whirlwind: *The 4 Disciplines of Execution®*

The 13 Behaviors that will Increase Engagement and Trust: Leading at the *Speed of Trust®*

Invest Your Time, Attention and Energy on Your Highest Priorities: *The 5 Choices to Extraordinary Productivity®*

Complete Your Projects on Time, on Budget, and on the Mark: *Project Management Essentials for the* Unofficial *Project Manager®*

Inspire Trust and Build Credibility as a Leader: *Leadership: Great Leaders, Great Teams, Great Results®*